GIRLZ ROCK

Other books in the growing Faithgirlz!™ library

Best Friends Bible

The Sophie Series

Sophie's World (Book One)
Sophie's Secret (Book Two)
Sophie and the Scoundrels (Book Three)
Sophie's Irish Showdown (Book Four)
Sophie's First Dance? (Book Five)
Sophie's Stormy Summer (Book Six)
Sophie Breaks the Code (Book Seven)
Sophie Tracks a Thief (Book Eight)

Nonfiction

No Boys Allowed: Devotions for Girls

Check out www.faithgirlz.com

faiThGirLz!™

GiRLz ROCK

DeVotions foR you

Written by Kristi Holl
with Jennifer Vogtlin

Zonderkidz

Zonderkidz.

The children's group of Zondervan

www.zonderkidz.com

Girlz Rock
Text copyright © 2005 by Kristi Holl

Requests for information should be addressed to:
Zonderkidz, 5300 Patterson Ave. SE, Grand Rapids, Michigan 49530

Library of Congress Cataloging-in-Publication Data

Holl, Kristi.
  Girlz rock / Kristi Holl with Jennifer Vogtlin.
  p. cm.– (Faithgirlz)
  ISBN-10: 0-310-70899-0 (softcover)
  ISBN-13: 978-0-310-70899-5 (softcover)
  1. Girls—Prayer-books and devotions—English. I. Vogtlin, Jennifer, 1976- II. Title. III.
Series.
  BV4860.H62 2005
  242'.62–dc22

                                                          2004028568

Scripture quotations come from the following sources:

The Amplified Bible, Old Testament. Copyright © 1965, 1987, by the Zondervan Corporation.
Used by permission. All rights reserved.

The Amplified Bible, New Testament. Copyright © 1954, 1958, 1987, by The Lockman Foundation. Used by permission.

HOLY BIBLE, NEW INTERNATIONAL VERSION®. Copyright © 1973, 1978, 1984 by International Bible Society. Used by permission of Zondervan. All rights reserved.

Holy Bible, New Living Translation. Scripture quotations marked (NLT) are taken from the *Holy Bible, New Living Translation,* copyright © 1996. Used by permission of Tyndale House Publishers, Inc., Wheaton, IL 60189 USA. All rights reserved.

THE MESSAGE. Copyright © by Eugene H. Peterson 1993, 1994, 1995, 1996, 2000, 2001, 2002. Used by permission of NavPress Publishing Group.

New American Standard Bible. Scripture taken from the New American Standard Bible, © Copyright 1960, 1962, 1963, 1968, 1971, 1972, 1973, 1975, 1977 by The Lockman Foundation. Used by permission.

The New King James Version. Scripture quotations marked "NKJV" are taken from the New King James Version. Copyright © 1982 by Thomas Nelson, Inc. Used by permission. All rights reserved.

Note abbreviations used herein, in alphabetical order: AMP, NIV, NLT, MSG, NASB, and NKJV. Also note that KJV means the King James Version of the Holy Bible.

Art Direction: Jody Langley
Interior design: Susan Ambs
Cover design: Gayle Raymer Design
Illustrated by: Robin Zingone

Printed in the United States

05 06 07 08 09 /❖DCI/ 5 4 3 2 1

Contents

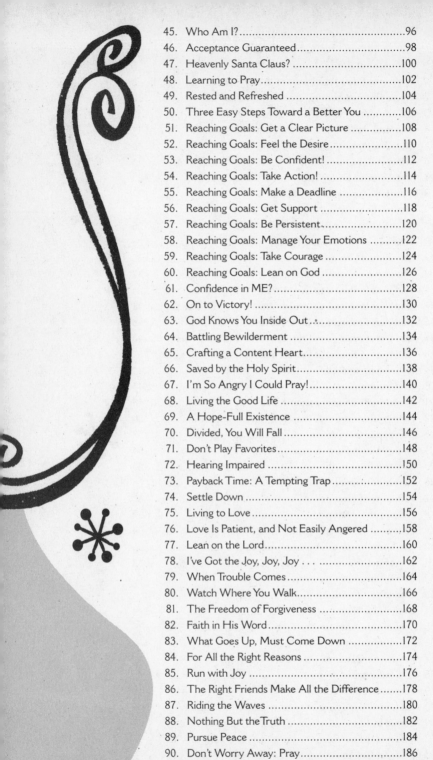

For Abby Dawn Vogtlin, with love from Nana.
How you've blessed my life!

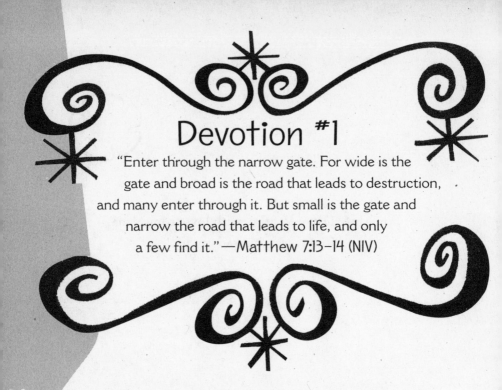

Devotion #1

"Enter through the narrow gate. For wide is the gate and broad is the road that leads to destruction, and many enter through it. But small is the gate and narrow the road that leads to life, and only a few find it." —Matthew 7:13–14 (NIV)

A Narrow Road That Leads To Wider Promise

You can enter God's kingdom only through the narrow gate that leads to life. The highway to hell is broad, and its gate is wide for the many who choose the easy way. But the road to life is narrow, and only a few ever find it.

Many of your friends will encourage you to join them on the wide path. It looks like fun, and Satan promises that you'll feel loved and accepted if you live as the world lives. You'll have more "friends" on the broad path. You won't be branded a "narrow-minded Christian" if you choose to travel on the Anything Goes Highway. On that wide path you'll hear that cheating to get good grades is okay, that R-rated movies don't hurt you, and that it's cool to drink and take drugs.

The broad way is also the way of disappointment and false promises. It can't deliver love and acceptance and long-lasting happiness because it's Satan's lie. Proverbs 16:25 (NKJV) says, "There is a way that seems right to a man, but its end is the way of death." The broad way might be "fun" for a while, but your heart will never find peace this way. True joy and acceptance are found through God on the narrow path. Traveling God's way can mean a difficult, rocky road at times. But it leads to peace here on earth and eternal life in heaven. It's not heavily traveled, but Jesus is always with you, so you're *never* alone.

You're standing at a fork in the road. Take off with confidence down the narrow way—to life!

Did You Know:

. . . that Jesus told the disciples they had to be like children (and have childlike faith) to enter heaven? Read Matthew 18:2–5.

More To Explore: Luke 13:24–25

Girl Talk:

What path are you walking on right now? Do you think God would be happy with your choices?

God Talk:

"Lord, I don't always make the right choices. Help me to be courageous and choose the right path. I want you to be proud of me. I love you. Amen."

Beauty 101:

Walking down a path is a great way to get exercise. Fast walking for twenty to thirty minutes a day gets your heart pumping. Walk only during the day, and take a buddy with you!

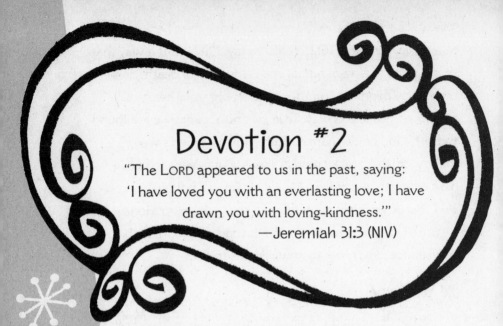

Devotion #2

"The LORD appeared to us in the past, saying:
'I have loved you with an everlasting love; I have
drawn you with loving-kindness.'"
—Jeremiah 31:3 (NIV)

Never-Ending Love

Our limited human minds find it hard to grasp how much God loves us. His love continues forever and can be counted on in all our times of need. God pulled us to him with his love and kindness. "We love Him because He first loved us" (1 John 4:19 NKJV).

Think about the person you love most in the world. Then multiply the love you feel for this person a thousand times. That's only a tiny drop of the love—the everlasting love—that God feels toward you.

Every day for a month, take a few minutes to think about how much God loves you. Say it out loud: "God loves *me*. The all-knowing, all-powerful, all-loving God of the universe loves *me*!" See how that changes your feelings during the month. We would live much differently if we truly understood how much God loves us. He wants only the best for us—all the time. He wants to meet all our needs—we only have to ask him. (That doesn't mean he will give you everything you *want*, but instead everything he knows you need.) He wants to fight our battles for us—we only have to lean on him. He wants to give us direction and to have the joy Jesus died for us to have.

God wanted us so much that he pulled us to him. Jesus said, "No one can come to me unless the Father who sent me draws him" (John 6:44 NIV). People do not come to Christ strictly because of their own ideas or decisions. It is God pulling them to him. He loves you and wants you that much!

God's love for you is without limit. Soak it up!

Did You Know ...

that God is faithful to those who love him? Moses tells the Israelites what will happen to them, depending on whether they love God or hate him. Read Deuteronomy 7:8–10 for more of the story.

Girl Talk:

Do you feel that God really loves you? How do you think he shows his love to you each day?

More To Explore: Psalm 103:17 and Titus 3:3–6

God Talk:

"Lord, it's hard to believe that you love me so much, but I am so grateful to have your love. Help me to show love to others the way you show your love for me. Thank you for never leaving me. Amen."

11

Devotion #3

"The good soil represents those who hear and accept God's message and produce a huge harvest—thirty, sixty, or even a hundred times as much as had been planted." —Mark 4:20 (NLT)

CULTIVATE YOUR FAITH

When you plant garden seeds, you don't expect much of a crop from dry, rocky ground, or a patch full of weeds. But good soil—black soil full of minerals—will produce up to a hundred times the amount of seed that was planted. In the same way, people with good hearts, ready to receive God's word and act on it, will also produce an abundant harvest. They will become all that God created them to be.

God has given you special talents and abilities that he wants you to use. Do you love to run fast? Do you have a good singing voice or an ability to play the flute well? Can you write poetry, or paint watercolors? God wants you to enjoy the gifts and talents, but also use them to bring joy to others and glory and praise to God. Is your life producing such a harvest? It can!

If you don't like your harvest, check your soil. Is it full of weeds (like resentment, laziness, or jealousy)? Then deal with the weeds. Pray for help to get rid of them, then do what God tells you to do. Is your soil dry and hard from lack of water (from ignoring reading your Bible)? Then soak it in the rivers of living water from God's Word. Then you'll grow the fruit of the Spirit: love, joy, peace, longsuffering, kindness, goodness, faithfulness, gentleness, and self-control (Galatians 5:22–23 NKJV).

If your soil needs attention, be a good farmer and plow it. Plant it with seeds of obedience to God's word—then wait for that bumper-crop harvest!

Did You Know ...

that an Academy Award-winning movie talked about using your talents for God? *Chariots of Fire* is a true story about English athletes in the 1920s. One of them, Eric Liddell, says, "I believe that God made me for a purpose, for China [as a missionary], but he also made me fast. And when I run, I feel his pleasure!"

Girl Talk:

Are you using your talents to the best of your ability? Can others see God's influence in your behavior?

More To Explore: Luke 8:15 and John 15:4–5

God Talk:

"Lord, I want to use my talents for you. Please help me to honor you in all I do. I want to give you a bumper crop! Amen."

Devotion #4

"Don't take pride in following a particular leader.
Everything belongs to you." —1 Corinthians 3:21 (NLT)

The Real "In" Group

Don't get your feelings of self-respect or personal
worth from being accepted by a particular person or group.
Because you belong to Christ, they don't have anything that
you don't have!

Most classes have a few girls who have decided they are the
"popular" group. They will claim to have inside information
that others don't have, or act as if they are more special than
anyone else. Don't fall for that! Don't believe the lie that
claims you have to be part of someone's group to be "in"
or "cool." You already belong to the coolest group
you could join: Father, Son, and Holy Spirit!
God designed you to have friendships
that are rewarding, with give-and-take
sharing. Relationships get out of balance
when one person thinks she is more special than others. YOU are important,
valuable, and significant. Centering your
life on someone who demands to be the

focus will throw your friendship out of balance.

If you belong to Christ (have accepted him as your Savior), then you're a daughter of the King. Everything God has belongs to Christ, and everything Jesus has is yours. If you stay true to him, all the blessings here and in eternity belong to you. You are as worthy as anyone else on earth—anyone! So don't brag about being part of So-and-So's group, or follow the "popular girls" because they have more of what the world offers. Your worth comes from belonging to Christ—not to a particular friend or group.

God says you have worth and value. You are worth so much to him that he sent his Son to die for you so that you could spend eternity with him. You can't get any more valuable than that!

Did You Know ...

that even a church with the great apostle Paul as teacher had problems with cliques? First Corinthians 1:10–13 describes the problem of a church in Corinth arguing over who was more important.

More To Explore: 1 Corinthians 3:3–6

Girl Talk:

Where do you go to feel wanted and respected? Do you rely on friends for self-esteem or God? You may rely on both, but always remember that God's opinion of you matters the most.

God Talk:

"Lord, I sometimes worry too much about what others think of me. Please help me remember that you are the one I need to please. In you, I have all the love and respect I will ever need! Thank you! Amen."

Devotion #5

"Obviously, I'm not trying to be a people pleaser!
No, I am trying to please God. If I were still trying to
please people, I would not be Christ's servant."
—Galatians 1:10 (NLT)

Be a God Pleaser!

Are you trying to win the approval and acceptance of
people? Is that your primary reason for saying and doing
things? You can't spend your time trying to win the approval
of people and still be a servant of Christ.

At the lunch table, when someone tells a dirty joke, do you
laugh too so you'll be accepted, even when the joke makes you
very uncomfortable? Or do you join in backbiting and gossip
about other students so you won't feel left out, even though
you know it's wrong? Do you ignore a less popular student because your friends would make fun of you if
you were kind to him? Then you are trying to
please people instead of God. And God's
Word says you can't be in God's service—
useful to him—if you're more interested
in people's opinions about you than God's.

As believers, we are to be like Christ
and follow in his footsteps. How did he
handle such situations? Once the Pharisees

tried to trap Jesus into saying something they could use against him. "'Teacher,' they said, 'we know you are a man of integrity and that you teach the way of God in accordance with the truth. You aren't swayed by men, because you pay no attention to who they are'" (Matthew 22:16 NIV). Jesus didn't play favorites or change what he said depending on who was listening. He said and did what God told him to say and do, no matter whom he was around. We are to be the same.

Go out and live your life today in a way that pleases God.

Did You Know ...

that even when you eat and drink, you can do it for the glory of God? In 1 Corinthians 10:31–33, Paul talks about doing everything for the glory of God, because you are always a witness to those around you.

More To Explore: Ephesians 6:5–8

Girl Talk:

When you think about doing something, do you only worry about others' reactions? Or do you also think about what God would say?

God Talk:

"Lord, I'm not always proud of the way I act, and I need your forgiveness. Help me to do what you would do, at all times. I want to be a great witness for you! Amen."

Devotion #6

"As the Father has loved me, so have I loved you. Now remain in my love." —John 15:9 (NIV)

Living in Love

Jesus wants you to know how much he loves you. Jesus said that he loves you just as God, the Father, loves him. Just as much, and in the same way. Imagine that! So it's important that you continue to rest and live in that everlasting, bountiful love.

Sometimes it's hard to believe God can love us that much. After all, we all do things that we know are wrong and for which we need forgiveness. Maybe you cheated and turned in a book report that you actually wrote last year. Perhaps you pretend to like your stepmother, but you secretly hate her. When you're so imperfect, can God still love you? YES! Or maybe your family is breaking up, or your health is breaking down. Does God still love you, no matter what is happening in your life? YES!

"I am convinced that nothing can ever separate us from his love. Death can't, and life can't. The angels can't, and the demons can't. Our fears for today, our worries about tomorrow, and even the powers of hell can't keep God's love away" (Romans 8:38 NLT).

Sometimes we need reminders that God loves us. Say it out loud: "God loves me, and I can trust him. God loves me, and I can trust him." If you have trouble believing that God really cares about you or that he can forgive you for your sins, repeat that to yourself several times every day for a month. Get it down deep inside you. In time, your love for others will also grow. "God is love, and all who live in love live in God, and God lives in them. And as we live in God, our love grows more perfect" (1 John 4:16–17 NLT).

Settle down, get comfortable, relax—and live in God's love for you.

Did You Know ...

that God's love surpasses all knowledge? Read Ephesians 3:17–19 and find out just how huge God's love is!

More To Explore: John 15:10–11 and Romans 5:6–8

Girl Talk:

Do you have days when you think that God can't possibly love you? Would it help you to remind yourself daily that God *does* love you?

God Talk:

"Lord, I know you love me so much that I can't understand it. Sometimes, I can't even believe it. Please help me to remember every day that you love me. Thank you for your love that never ends. Amen."

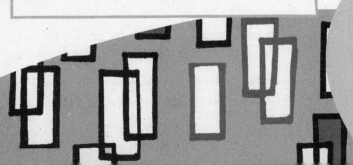

Devotion #7

"So we say with confidence, 'The Lord is my helper;
I will not be afraid. What can man do to me?'"
—Hebrews 13:6 (NIV)

Your Personal Bodyguard

As we look at events in our lives, God's Word says
that we can be confident. Why? Because the almighty,
all-loving Lord is our helper. So we don't need to be worried
or insecure. With the all-powerful God on our side, what can
people do to us?

Bullies are a nasty reality of life sometimes. A bully may be
a bossy older brother who dominates the house when your
parents are at work. It can be a cruel teacher or coach who
discourages with his comments. A brutal kid on the
school bus or playground may threaten you with
physical harm. Life can be *scary* sometimes.

We may think bullies are a modern thing.
We might even think that God doesn't
understand our situation. But see David's
words in the Psalms (don't his words
sound like today?): "In God (I will praise
His word), in God I have put my trust; I
will not fear. What can flesh do to me? All

day they twist my words; all their thoughts are against me for evil. They gather together, they hide, they mark my steps, when they lie in wait for my life" (Psalm 56:4–6 NKJV). Threatening bullies have been around for thousands of years!

You may be powerless to deal with them on your own, but with God on your side, the Bible says you don't have to be afraid. So how do you find this courage and help? Go to God in prayer. "Let us therefore come boldly to the throne of grace, that we may obtain mercy and find grace to help in time of need" (Hebrews 4:16 NKJV).

Pray. Believe God will help you. Watch for it. Say boldly, "I will not fear!"

Did You Know ...

that Sophie feels threatened by Julia and friends in *Sophie's Secret*? Read to find out how Sophie deals with it.

God Talk:

"Lord, sometimes other people are trying to scare me. You are my rock and my refuge. Please deliver me from their words and actions. Thank you. Amen."

More To Explore: Deuteronomy 33:27 and Psalm 56:11

Girl Talk:

Do you ever feel bullied by others? Have you ever asked God to deliver you from them?

Fun Factoid:

David calls God many different names that deal with shelter and protection. He calls God a rock, a fortress, a refuge, a shield, a deliverer, and a stronghold. Read Psalms 18:1–2; 31:2–3; 71:3; and 94:22.

Devotion #8

"The strong spirit of a man sustains him in bodily pain or trouble, but a weak and broken spirit who can raise up or bear?" —Proverbs 18:14 (AMP)

Strength Training for Your Spirit

Everyone will experience sickness or trouble sometimes, but if your spirit is strong, you can face it and survive. But someone with a weak or wounded spirit finds it nearly impossible to bear up under anything. Their problems may not be worse than anyone else's, but they won't be strong enough to endure or overcome their difficulties.

Haven't you noticed this difference in yourself? On Monday, when you're confident inside and someone calls you a stupid name, you shrug it off. You know that the problem is with the other person, not you. But if it happens again on Wednesday, when you feel weaker inside, the same remark makes you cry. Sometimes you know the cause of feeling "down" (a bad grade, overhearing a fight between your parents, the flu), but some days there seems to be no reason. When your spirit is weak, it's hard to overcome or endure anything with the right attitude.

So what can you do? First, you must learn

to encourage yourself. There won't always be someone around to do it for you. David learned this too and wrote, "Why are you downcast, O my soul? Why so disturbed within me? Put your hope in God, for I will yet praise him, my Savior and my God" (Psalm 42:11 NIV). He talked to himself! He said, "Hey, mind and emotions, what's the matter with you? Why are you down in the dumps? Put your hope in God, not these circumstances, and praise him!" David had learned to encourage himself.

Then encourage others when you see that they need a kind or uplifting word. Be the kind of girl people love to see coming because they feel better every time you're around. "We urge you, brothers, . . . encourage the timid, help the weak, be patient with everyone" (1 Thessalonians 5:14 NIV).

Be strong in spirit, and you can handle anything!

Did You Know ...

that Sophie's spirit feels weak during a tough week in *Sophie's Secret*? She calls it No-God space. Read to see how she handles it.

Girl Talk:

Are there days when your spirit feels stronger and more confident? Or weaker and easily hurt? Do you ask God for help?

God Talk:

"Lord, sometimes my spirit gets hurt so easily. Please help me to rely on you, not on others. I want my hope to stay in you! Amen."

More To Explore: Psalm 51:10–12 and 1 Peter 1:3–7

Devotion #9

"Blessed is the man you discipline, O LORD, the
man you teach from your law; you grant him relief
from days of trouble, till a pit is dug for the wicked."
—Psalm 94:12–13 (NIV)

How To Stay Calm, No Matter What

The person whom God corrects, trains, and teaches is
happy and very fortunate. This person is given rest and relief
from troubled times. God gives him the "power to keep himself calm in the days of adversity" (Psalm 94:13 AMP).

Some problems are over quickly, but some seem to drag on
and on. Maybe your mom has a serious illness that requires con-
stant medical attention. Or you have an older brother who
gets in scrapes with the police and embarrasses you at school
and church. You want relief from your day of trouble—
and the ability to be at peace until it's over.

Wouldn't you *love* to have the power to stay
calm, no matter what happened? You can
have this power! Just don't miss the part
that has to come first. Before the power
comes, God uses the events and people
in our lives to build our spiritual character.
For example, he may teach you about the
power of prayer during your mom's illness.

He wants us to be calm and steadfast. After being taught by God, we become stable, happy, and powerful. Then we can remain calm and steady while we wait for our troubles to work out.

Why is God's discipline good? (It sure doesn't FEEL good sometimes!) This is what David said about it: "I used to wander off until you disciplined me; but now I closely follow your word. You are good and do only good; teach me your principles" (Psalm 119:67–68 NLT).

God's discipline keeps you on the narrow path, where he knows the biggest blessings await you.

Did You Know ...

that God disciplines us because he loves us so much? He wants what is best for us. Read Proverbs 3:11–12 to learn more.

Girl Talk:

When you face problems, do you want them over right now? Have you ever thought that God gives you problems because he loves you?

God Talk:

"Lord, it's hard to wait for my problems to be over. Help me to remember that you send trials my way in order for me to grow. Thank you for loving me so much! Amen."

More To Explore: Job 5:17 and Psalm 119:71

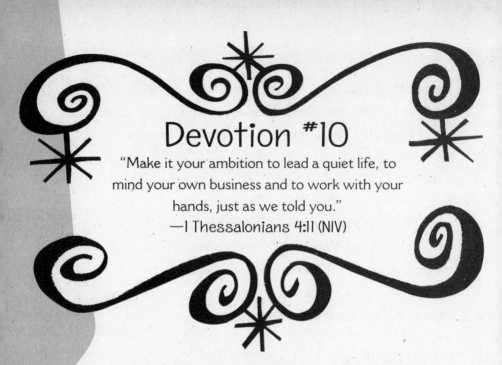

Devotion #10

"Make it your ambition to lead a quiet life, to mind your own business and to work with your hands, just as we told you."
—1 Thessalonians 4:11 (NIV)

Become Busy, Not a Busybody

Your desire or goal should be to lead a life that is free from turmoil and emotional upset. Be calm and well-balanced. One way to do this is by paying attention to (and taking care of) your own business. Don't go poking your nose into other people's personal matters.

When friends ask you how much you paid for something, or dig through your purse or backpack to see what's in there, or ask how much you weigh, your first instinct is to say, "Hey, mind your own business!" Feel free, in a kind tone of voice, to say just that. People need to pay attention to their own concerns instead of nosing around in other people's business. (If you want to tell your friends a private detail, that's one thing. But they *don't* have a right to know just because they are nosy enough to ask.) It goes both ways too. No matter how curious you feel about another person's private life, mind your own business. Instead, work on your jobs at home or school.

The Greeks felt that manual labor (working with your hands) was degrading and only for slaves. But the Bible makes it clear that all honest work is godly. If you're working hard on the things you need to do, you won't have time to be nosy. "We hear that some among you are idle. They are not busy; they are busybodies" (2 Thessalonians 3:11 NIV). Idleness (not working) often leads to this problem. People who are paying attention to their own jobs, families, schoolwork, and church activities rarely have time to be nosy.

Let other people mind their own affairs while you pay attention to yours. Everyone will benefit!

Did You Know ...

that Peter puts being a busybody in the same category as thieves and murderers?! Read 1 Peter 4:15.

God Talk:

"Lord, I thank you that I have friends who are interested in me. Please help me tell the difference between true caring and prying. I want to have true friends and be one myself. Thank you. Amen."

More To Explore: 1 Timothy 5:13

Girl Talk:

When you are with your friends or classmates, can you be open with them? Do they try to find out every private thing about you? If so, what could you say to them?

Fun Factoid:

Sophie gets really upset over what some of the class busybodies do. See what happens to her in *Sophie's Secret*.

Devotion #11

"You need to persevere so that when you have done the will of God, you will receive what he has promised." —Hebrews 10:36 (NIV)

Promises Worth Waiting For

You need to have patience and stick to your plan of action, no matter how long something takes. Why? So that (after you have done what God commanded) you will receive all of what he promised to give you.

TV shows, movies, and magazines cry, "Get it now!" It might be an instant meal, instant cash, or instant get-rich-quick wealth. God's Word says the opposite. He gives a specific promise or a general principle and tells you how to obtain it. After you've done what God said, there might be a waiting period before the promise appears. God uses that waiting period to "grow you up" spiritually, developing character qualities that will benefit you all your life.

What things has God promised to give believers? Everything from love and peace to eternal life. He also gives us wise principles to live by. For example, if you need money, check out these ideas (and see what God tells *you* to do): "A generous man will prosper; he who refreshes others will himself be refreshed" (Proverbs 11:25 NIV). And "Whoever sows generously will also reap generously" (2 Corinthians 9:6 NIV). And "All hard work brings a profit, but mere talk leads only to poverty" (Proverbs 14:23 NIV). Your part? Work hard and be generous. Be persistent. Practicing these principles over time can turn your circumstances around.

Being patient is *not* the ability to sit calmly and do nothing, waiting for something to happen. Patient perseverance, the kind needed to receive God's promises, is very active. It is the ability to hang tough when it gets hard, when you want to take a shortcut to get what you want.

Instead, "rest in the LORD, and wait patiently for Him" (Psalm 37:7 NKJV). Your promise is on its way!

Did You Know ...

that Hebrews 6:10–12 encourages us to be diligent and not become lazy? It also mentions having faith and patience.

God Talk:

"Lord, it's hard for me to be patient. Help me to remember that my answer is on its way. Thank you for meeting my needs. Amen."

Girl Talk:

Is it hard for you to wait for something you want or need? Do you talk to God about it?

More To Explore: Psalm 40:1 and Matthew 21:28–31

Fun Factoid:

Did you know that *patience* and other forms of the word, like *patient*, are mentioned forty-seven times in the Bible? Having patience seems to be pretty important in God's eyes!

Devotion #12

"Only simpletons believe everything they are told!
The prudent carefully consider their steps."
—Proverbs 14:15 (NLT)

Uncommon Common Sense

Some people are without common sense and lack knowledge of the world. These inexperienced people will believe anything they're told and follow along blindly. A wise, sensible person, however, shows good judgment and self-control. This person gives very careful thought before taking any action and avoids much trouble.

How many of the following statements have you wrongly believed? "Hey, let's cut science class and go to the mall 'cause that teacher never takes attendance." Or "Just loan me your ten dollars, and I'll pay you back fifteen on Friday." Or "You're so brilliant, and I just don't get this math. Can you do it for me?"

Sometimes we mistakenly think that it's not Christian to doubt someone's word or question things we're told. We've read that being suspicious is a sin, so we hide our misgivings and give the other person the benefit of the doubt. Believing everything you're told is a good way to get into trouble; you must find balance. If something sounds fishy or too good to be true, take a step back, because it probably is. You don't have to snarl, "I know you're lying!" (That's not speaking the truth in love.) But don't agree too quickly, either, and don't make commitments you'll regret later. Always talk to the Lord about your misgivings and those "funny feelings in the pit of your stomach." The Holy Spirit may be trying to get your attention so you can steer clear of danger or avoid making a bad decision. Romans 16:17–18 (NKJV) says to "avoid . . . those who . . . by smooth words and flattering speech deceive the hearts of the simple."

Be wise. Examine what people tell you. Then give careful thought to what you should do.

Did You Know . . .

that Paul told the churches to be wary of any who said things that conflicted with the gospel? He said even if angels are speaking contrary things, they should be cursed! Read Galatians 1:8.

Girl Talk:

Do you tend to believe everything you're told? Do you ask questions and try to find out the real story? Do you ever get that "funny feeling" in your stomach telling you something's not right?

More To Explore: Proverbs 22:3 and Ephesians 4:14

God Talk:

"Lord, I'm glad that I have friends to talk with. Please give me wisdom to know who is truthful and to avoid those who lie. Help me to be truthful at all times. Thank you. Amen."

Devotion #13

"The good man brings good things out of the good stored up in his heart, and the evil man brings evil things out of the evil stored up in his heart. For out of the overflow of his heart his mouth speaks."
—Luke 6:45 (NIV)

The Heart of the Matter

Whatever is truly in your heart will come out in your words and actions. You can't pretend for long. If you have a heart full of good, you'll produce good deeds and say good things. If evil words and actions flow from a person, it's because he has evil stored in his heart instead. Whatever is in your heart determines what you say.

When your little brother chatters nonstop on the way to school, do you say, "That sounds interesting," or "Shut up, twerp"? When a gossip session at lunch is tearing down a teacher, do you join in or find something positive to say? When you have to wait in line forever to buy something, do you say, "Have a nice day" to the clerk—or "My grandma moves faster than you do"? Whatever comes out of your mouth reveals the condition of your heart.

There shouldn't be a mixture—some good, some bad—coming out of our mouths. However, oftentimes there is. Even if 90 percent of what you say is positive and good, there might be a particular person or situation that continually tempts you to say things that aren't godly. If so, take the matter to God. Ask him to reveal whatever unforgiving thoughts or bitterness lives in your heart, and deal with it. Read Psalm 51, and confess whatever needs confessing. "Create in me a pure heart, O God, and renew a steadfast spirit within me" (v. 10 NIV). Your mouth is like a barometer of your heart, measuring and revealing its condition, so pay attention to your words.

Feed your heart a steady diet of the Word of God. Then watch your mouth become a fountain of blessings for everyone you meet!

Did You Know ...

that a person who deceives may have "speech smoother than oil," but in the end, she is as "sharp as a double-edged sword"? Don't let your actions be lethal weapons! Read Proverbs 5:1–4.

More To Explore: Psalm 37:30–31

Girl Talk:

Do you watch the words that come out of your mouth? What situations are the hardest for you?

God Talk:

"Lord, I have good intentions, but I don't always say nice things. Please help me to think before I speak. I want to say what you would say. Thank you! Amen."

Devotion #14

"No discipline seems pleasant at the time, but painful.
Later on, however, it produces a harvest of righteousness
and peace for those who have been trained by it."
—Hebrews 12:11 (NIV)

God Uses Problems To Direct You

We don't enjoy discipline while it's happening—it's painful! Being trained in self-control is hard! But afterward, you will have peace and the blessings of right living reserved for those who are trained in this way.

Morgan knew she'd overeaten all summer, but it wasn't until she bought new school clothes that she realized how much weight she'd gained. Not being able to buy the cute clothes she saw was hard enough, but returning to school was worse. Girls in gym class raced circles around her. Climbing stairs between classes left her winded. Worst of all, her muscles were so weak that she couldn't finish her gymnastics workouts, and she got dropped from the team.

Discipline often comes in the form of problems we want to hide from. We often fail to see how God is trying to use *those very problems* to help us learn more about ourselves. Take time to pray and consider how God might be using that problem to benefit you. Remember that "the Lord disciplines those he loves" (Hebrews 12:6 NIV), and "God disciplines us for our good" (Hebrews 12:10 NIV).

Sometimes it takes a painful situation for God to get our attention. He may want to turn you in a different direction or motivate you to make a change in your life. Losing her place on the gymnastics team was painful for Morgan. However, it motivated her to take better care of her body, which is the temple of the Holy Spirit.

Developing self-control is hard, but remember the rewards! Stay focused on the prize you'll receive at the end.

Did You Know ...

that "he who hates correction will die"? People like this will keep making bad choices until one of those choices kills them. Read Proverbs 15:10.

Girl Talk:

How do you handle being disciplined? Can you understand why you need to be corrected from time to time? Do you see why God wants to correct you?

More To Explore: Hebrews 12:5–6 and 2 Corinthians 4:17

God Talk:

"Lord, being corrected is not my favorite thing. I usually get really upset. Please help me to remember that you discipline me because you love me. You want what is best for me. Thank you for loving me that much! Amen."

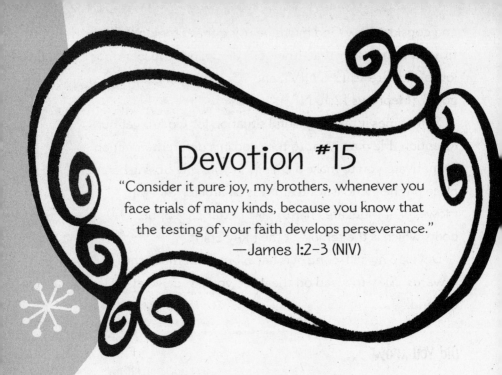

Devotion #15

"Consider it pure joy, my brothers, whenever you
face trials of many kinds, because you know that
the testing of your faith develops perseverance."
—James 1:2–3 (NIV)

God Uses Problems To Inspect You

Whenever trouble of any kind comes your way, let it be an opportunity for joy. Problems test our faith to see what it's really made of. Problems and tests also give our endurance and patience a chance to grow.

It's easy to believe we trust God, and to look like our faith is strong, when we don't have any problems. But problems are what tests our faith, to reveal what's really inside us. People are like tea bags. If you want to know what's inside, drop them into hot water! Your faith is like that. When faced with a problem—an angry stepdad, a sprained ankle before the track meet, money shortages—how's your faith? Are you still confident that God will meet all your needs? Do you wait patiently for God's answers and help? Until you've seen God supply your needs and help you through a few problems, it can be extremely hard to view problems as opportunities for joy. But "blessed is the man who perseveres under trial, because when he has stood the test, he will receive the crown of life that God has promised to those who love him" (James 1:12 NIV). Once your faith has endured a few tests, you will view problems differently. You will know a blessing waits for you after you face the trial successfully. Usually, the bigger the test, the bigger the reward for keeping your faith in God strong.

Whatever trial or problem you're facing today, thank God for the opportunity to grow stronger in your faith. Keep trusting God, and it will happen!

Did You Know ...

that your faith is far more precious to God than gold? Read 1 Peter 1:6–8 to learn the relation between trials of faith and gold.

Girl Talk:

Have you ever thought of problems as a chance to grow? Do you stay close to God during trials?

More To Explore: Romans 8:17–18 and 1 Peter 4:13

God Talk:

"Lord, I am learning that trials are a chance to grow in my faith. Please help me to remember that. Thank you for always being with me. Amen."

Fun Factoid:

In the entire world, the total amount of gold is about the size of a forty-four-foot cube. That's about a trillion dollars worth!

Devotion #16

"The suffering you sent was good for me, for it taught me to pay attention to your principles."
—Psalm 119:71 (NLT)

God Uses Problems To Connect You

Pain hurts at the time we feel it, but it's good for us if it teaches us to pay attention to God's rules for our personal behavior. Unhappiness and distress feel bad, but when the suffering teaches us something as valuable as God's rules for living, the pain is a blessing in disguise.

Anna refused to wear her helmet; then she received a concussion when her bike skidded in gravel and she crashed. Sarah refused to go to bed on time and talked on the phone until midnight on school nights, then was sick and missed an outing to the water park. Kate went to the mall when she was supposed to be studying, resulting in her having no money for things she needed—and failing several tests.

Each girl had plenty of problems and pain to work through, but (in the end) Anna began wearing her helmet, Sarah started getting enough sleep, and Kate studied during the school week instead of shopping. Their lives were much more successful. Their problems were blessings in disguise.

Some lessons we learn only through pain and failure. When you were very young, your parents probably told you not to touch the hot stove, but you *learned* not to do it by being burned once. Sometimes, unfortunately, we only learn the true value of something—health, money, a friendship—by losing it, at least long enough to feel some pain. "I used to wander off until you disciplined me; but now I closely follow your word. You are good and do only good; teach me your principles" (Psalm 119:67–68 NLT).

The next time you face a problem, pray and ask God if he is trying to teach you something. Listen for his answer. Then obey yourself right out of the problem!

Did You Know ...

that God doesn't want us condemned with the rest of the world? He disciplines us so that we can become better and better; in the world, but not of it. Read 1 Corinthians 11:32.

More To Explore: Psalm 94:12

Girl Talk:

Think back to a time when you made a wrong choice. What were the consequences? Do you think God was teaching you something?

God Talk:

"Lord, I sometimes make sinful choices and unwise choices. Please help me to see what I did wrong, so that I don't do it again. I want to learn and grow. Amen."

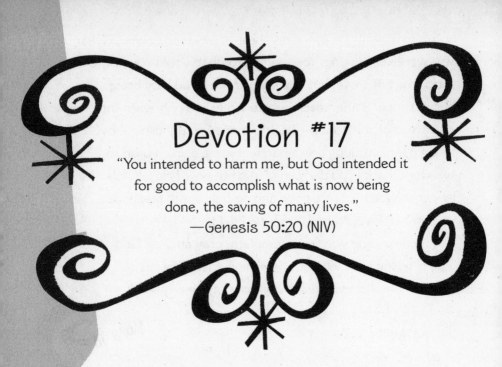

Devotion #17

"You intended to harm me, but God intended it
for good to accomplish what is now being
done, the saving of many lives."
—Genesis 50:20 (NIV)

God Uses Problems To Protect You

As far as Joseph was concerned, God turned into good
what his brothers meant for evil. Joseph's brothers, out of
jealousy, sold him into slavery. But their betrayal was used by
God to put Joseph in a place of power in Egypt. God brought
Joseph to that high position so he could save the lives of many
people during a famine when there was a severe shortage of
food. God brought good out of the evil. He still works like
this in the lives of believers.

Jenny's feelings were terribly hurt when her best
friend dumped her because Jenny wouldn't
shoplift a bracelet "just for fun." Six months
later, Jenny was grateful to God that she
wasn't at the mall with her friend when
she was arrested for theft. The friendship
was broken to protect Jenny. Alyssa was
hurt that her parents didn't seem to trust
her—they wouldn't let her ride to school with

the teenage neighbor boy. But when he totaled his car while speeding, Alyssa was grateful that God used her parents' *no!* to protect her. Sometimes we have friendship problems, and no matter what we do, the friendship dies. Perhaps God knows that down the road, being friends with that person would do you much damage.

God used a painful problem (Joseph's being sold into slavery) to save Joseph and many others from a worse problem: death during a famine. So when you face a problem or a disappointment, take time to pray. Ask God if he is perhaps trying to protect you from serious pain in the future. Then give him your thanks and praise!

Did You Know ...

that David called the Lord "my hiding place"? God was his safe zone! Read Psalm 32:7 for more.

God Talk:

"Lord, I sometimes don't understand why you send problems my way. Please help me to know whether you are trying to protect me. Thank you for your perfect wisdom in my life. Amen."

Girl Talk:

When you look back at past problems, did God do you a favor by allowing some trouble into your life? Can you see any results now that you couldn't see then?

More To Explore: Proverbs 2:8

41

Devotion #18

"We can rejoice, too, when we run into problems
and trials, for we know that they are good for us—
they help us learn to endure. And endurance
develops strength of character in us."
—Romans 5:3–4 (NLT)

God Uses Problems To Perfect You

We can have joy even in the middle of problems and pain. We aren't happy *because* we have problems, but because we know the suffering has a purpose. Part of God's purpose is to produce character in his children. And he knows that problems help us learn to endure, to hang in there when things are hard. This endurance builds strong qualities that will help us make good, moral decisions in life.

However, the problems themselves don't build character. (We all know people whose problems have made them depressed and bitter.) *Responding correctly* to problems is what develops a godly character.

Beth and Rosa both had mean stepfathers they didn't like. Rosa refused to do things he asked, got into yelling matches, and ended up running away from home. Beth's stepfather was just as difficult to get along with, but she chose to respond to her situation differently. She knew that God's Word says, "Love your enemies! Pray for those who persecute you!" (Matthew 5:44 NLT). Beth decided to be quiet, but pray for her stepfather's heart to be softened. It didn't happen overnight—it took endurance on Beth's part—but within a year she and her stepfather were spending time together fishing. Two situations—two very different responses—and two very different outcomes. Beth chose to allow her problem to help her grow.

We start out as spiritual babies, and we need to grow up. If we always got everything we wanted, when we wanted it, we'd be spoiled and remain babies. For that reason, God allows problems and trials into our lives.

The next time you face a problem, be determined to learn from it. Let God use it to perfect your character.

Did You Know ...

that discipline can produce a "harvest of righteousness and peace"? Hebrews 12:10–11 talks about how God disciplines us for our good.

God Talk:

"Lord, I want to do what you would do when a problem comes my way. Help me to remember you are testing me to make my faith grow. Thank you for your interest and love for me. Amen."

More To Explore:

Girl Talk:

Think of a problem you are facing now, whether big or small. If you didn't know about God's Word, what would you do about the problem? How would God say to respond?

Matthew 5:10–12 and 2 Corinthians 4:17

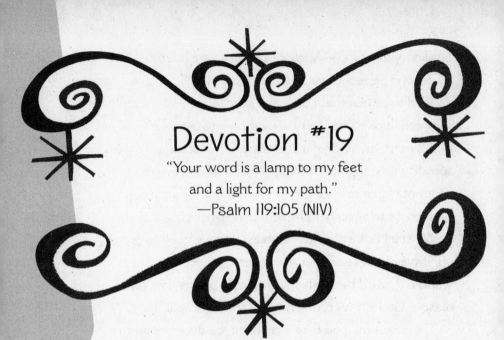

Devotion #19

"Your word is a lamp to my feet
and a light for my path."
—Psalm 119:105 (NIV)

Illuminating Your Life

We're all on a journey through life. It can be dark and confusing at times. But God's Word—the principles and commandments in it—light the way. It makes the narrow path visible, so we don't have to stumble and fall. Lamps and lights also serve as warning signals, like when a bridge is out. In the same manner, God's Word acts as a signal, warning us away from trouble.

Amber is a new girl in the sixth grade who wants to make friends. Should she choose the plain girl who is calm, or the flashy, fun-looking girl who often displays a short temper? If Amber looks in God's Word, it will shine a light on her path. "Do not make friends with a hot-tempered man, do not associate with one easily angered" (Proverbs 22:24 NIV). How about Heather? She doesn't know how to handle a bully in her gym class who insults her. If she wants to make a wise decision, she'll let God's Word shine a light on her situation. "A fool shows his annoyance at once, but a prudent [sensible] man overlooks an insult" (Proverbs 12:16 NIV).

Maybe you can't find a specific Bible verse to cover your situation. If not, pray and ask God for his advice. He promises to give it to you. James 1:5 (NLT) says, "If you need wisdom—if you want to know what God wants you to do—ask him, and he will gladly tell you. He will not resent your asking." Sometimes you can sense the answer right away, and sometimes you have to wait for a while before you know what to do. But God *will* answer. "You will light my lamp; the LORD my God will enlighten my darkness" (Psalm 18:28 NKJV).

Put an end to the darkness on your path through life. Turn on the Light!

Did You Know ...

that David thought the commands of the Lord were "radiant"? Psalm 19:8 says God's commands help you see the right path to take, giving you "light."

More To Explore: Proverbs 6:23 and Job 29:2–3

Girl Talk:

When you have a problem, do you do what *you* want to do? Or do you ask God what *he* wants you to do?

God Talk:

"Lord, I don't always wait for you to tell me what to do. Help me to stop and pray about my problems before I do anything. I know what you want for me is best. Thank you. Amen."

Devotion #20

"Remember that the temptations that come into your life are no different from what others experience. And God is faithful. He will keep the temptation from becoming so strong that you can't stand up against it. When you are tempted, he will show you a way out so that you will not give in to it." —1 Corinthians 10:13 (NLT)

Stand Strong

We all want to have—or do—something that we know we should avoid. Everyone experiences temptation of one kind or another, and the temptation itself is NOT a sin. It's only a test. God is always there for you. Turn to him, and ask for help. God won't let the test, or temptation, get too strong for you to fight. Also, he will show you a way out so you don't have to give in to it.

Temptations come in all sizes. Your older sister left her wallet on the table, and you're tempted to take a little of her money. Your friend hurt you, and you're tempted to gossip about her to anyone who will listen. The Bible says that temptations happen to all people. God won't shield you from all temptation, but he won't let it overpower you. He'll give you a way out if you really want to overcome it.

Sometimes you need to get away from the temptation. If you're tempted to buy too much candy, leave the store. If you're tempted to take money, remember these words and get away: "The love of money is a root of all kinds of evil, for which some have strayed from the faith in their greediness . . . But you, O man of God, flee these things and pursue righteousness, godliness, faith, love, patience, gentleness" (1 Timothy 6:10–11 NKJV). No matter what test you face, God will be faithful in each and every one. He'll show you a way out.

So stand strong in the Lord!

Did You Know ...

that many verses talk about the Lord rescuing and protecting us? Here are just three of them: 2 Peter 2:9; 2 Timothy 4:18; and 2 Thessalonians 3:3.

Girl Talk:

What are some things that tempt you? What do you do when they are staring you in the face? What do you think God wants you to do?

More To Explore: Luke 22:31–32 and Ephesians 6:12–13

God Talk:

"Lord, when I see _____, I feel really tempted. I know I shouldn't do it, but it is hard to resist. Help me to resist these temptations and rely on you for all my needs. Thank you for never leaving my side! Amen."

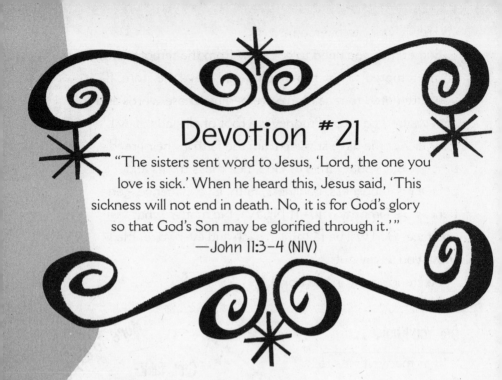

Devotion #21

"The sisters sent word to Jesus, 'Lord, the one you love is sick.' When he heard this, Jesus said, 'This sickness will not end in death. No, it is for God's glory so that God's Son may be glorified through it.'"
—John 11:3-4 (NIV)

Dealing With Disappointment

Martha, Mary, and their brother (Lazarus) were Jesus' very close friends. So when they sent urgent word to Jesus that Lazarus was deathly sick, they were terribly disappointed and hurt when Jesus didn't hurry to their home and heal him. Jesus loved them, but he waited two days to respond. Mary and Martha had no idea that God was planning something even greater than healing Lazarus. He was going to raise him from the dead!

We all are disappointed at times by those we love. Caitlin's best friend promised to stay overnight on Friday, but she forgot and went shopping with her sister instead. Nicole pleaded with her dad for help on her science project, but by the time he was available, the deadline was past. Samantha prayed that they wouldn't have to move, but her dad got transferred anyway.

We need to remember that God knows more about every situation than we do. When we are very disappointed, we need to remind ourselves that God knows *everything*. It's like we're standing on a street corner, watching a parade. We can only see the float or band that's right in front of us. But God is like the TV cameraman high up on the corner of the roof who looks down and can see the whole parade: beginning, middle, and end. Mary and Martha could only see that their brother had died. But Jesus knew the ending—that he was going to raise Lazarus from the dead and display God's power.

The next time you're disappointed, trust that God knows more about the situation than you do. He has a much better plan in mind!

Did You Know ...

that God tells us straight-out that he doesn't think like us? In Isaiah 55:8–9, God says that our ways are not his ways, meaning that we can't understand what he's going to do. But we do know that we can trust him!

More To Explore: Romans 8:28

Girl Talk:

Who has disappointed you in the recent past? Did you rely on yourself (or on God) to cheer up? Have you disappointed anyone lately? If so, ask their forgiveness.

God Talk:

"Lord, sometimes I feel hurt by the way others treat me. Help me to let go of my hurt feelings and to rely on you for my happiness. Thank you for never failing me! Amen."

Devotion #22

"They are all around me with their hateful words, and they fight against me for no reason. I love them, but they try to destroy me—even as I am praying for them!"

—Psalm 109:3-4 (NLT)

Fighting Back with . . . Prayer?

Sometimes, for no reason, people will make false accusations against you. People like to slander and gossip, and you may be the target sometimes. Even when you treat them right, they may be hateful in return. Your response to that? Be in prayer for them and about the situation.

Heather couldn't understand why the girls in her gym class chose her to ridicule or call names. Heather wasn't any plumper or clumsier or slower than anyone else. Maria's own mother attacked her with hateful words too—at home. Her mom was miserable at work and going through a divorce; no matter how hard Maria tried, her mom poured out her anger and frustration on Maria. Heather decided to fight back, and the situation in gym worsened as the girls called one another names. Maria prayed nightly instead, and God comforted her, although her mom didn't change for months.

Even when you are trying to do everything right, there may be some people in your life who are nasty and hateful, slandering you for no reason. It can be classmates, kids at church, even people within your own family. It's very sad, but it does sometimes happen. The psalmist said he loved and prayed for those mean-spirited people, but they fought him anyway.

Why does it happen? Sometimes others can misunderstand the things you do. And you can't please people all the time, no matter how hard you try. Instead, do what you believe will please *God* and is right in his eyes. Then pray about any bad, hateful reactions you get from others.

No matter how others act, choose to show them love and pray for them. God will richly bless you for it.

Did You Know ...

that Jesus was wrongly accused of evil deeds? Jesus claimed to be God, and the Jews thought him the worst kind of liar. Read John 10:22–32.

Girl Talk:

Are there any people in your life who are determined to be nasty? How do you respond? Do you fight back or rely on God?

God Talk:

"Lord, I don't know how to deal with _____. I want to respond the way Jesus would. Help me to focus on you and not on fighting back. Thank you. Amen."

More To Explore: 1 Samuel 19:4–5 and Psalm 35:19–23

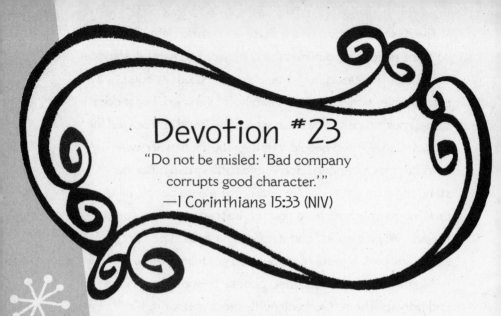

Devotion #23

"Do not be misled: 'Bad company
corrupts good character.'"
—1 Corinthians 15:33 (NIV)

Don't Lose Yourself

Don't be fooled into thinking that it doesn't matter
what kinds of friends you have. Hanging out with
immoral and dishonest friends can change you! They can
ruin your good habits, morals, and godly character.

Megan's mom was worried about the new friends Megan
made at school. Two of the girls were constantly in the principal's office for mouthing off to teachers. One friend had been
suspended for shoplifting. Megan assured her mom that she'd
never do such things, and she was telling the truth. She
honestly had no intention of becoming like those girls.
They just had money to spend and were a lot of
fun. A few months later, Megan was using the
same bad language at school and occupying
her own seat in the principal's office.

Sometimes believers think that they
can hang out with dishonest or immoral
friends because Jesus did it. After all, he
hung out with thieving tax collectors and

prostitutes. Shouldn't we do the same thing so that we can be good witnesses to them? Yes, and no. There is a difference between talking with "bad company" and choosing them for your closest friends.

Consider this example. When you mix a glass of pure, clean water with a glass of dirty water, it all becomes dirty and cloudy. The dirt spreads—not the purity. If you're healthy when you sit next to a very sick person, you can catch his flu, but he won't catch your health. In the same way, bad company is "catching."

Do be friendly with everyone, but choose moral girls with good character for your closest friends. Then you can build one another up and grow in godly character together.

Did You Know ...

that Timothy compared godless chatter to gangrene? Gangrene occurs when tissue on your body begins to rot because there is no blood supply. Timothy is saying that talking godlessly kills off your morals bit by bit. Read 2 Timothy 2:16–17.

More To Explore: Proverbs 13:20

Girl Talk:

Who are your closest friends? How do they behave? How do you behave when you are with them?

God Talk:

"Lord, I want to make good choices when making friends. Help me to find those who have good character and who want to get closer to you. Thank you. Amen."

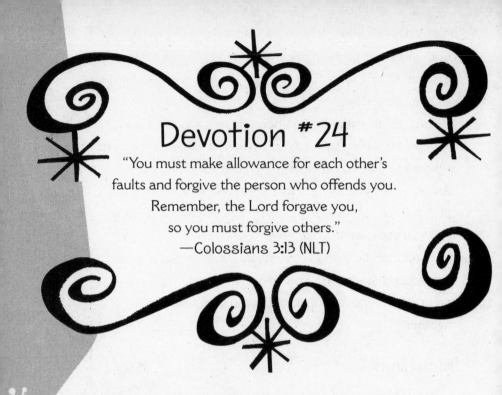

Devotion #24

"You must make allowance for each other's
faults and forgive the person who offends you.
Remember, the Lord forgave you,
so you must forgive others."
—Colossians 3:13 (NLT)

Find a Way To Forgive

You need to patiently put up with others' faults. Forgive
any grudges or resentments you're carrying about another
person. Remember how much the Lord has forgiven you! You
must do likewise, and forgive others.

We have to forgive our family members for their faults
many times each week. Your dad might be forgetful, and he
doesn't remember your birthday until he sees the cake
on the supper table. Your sister tends to gossip, and
she tells her boyfriend about the test you failed.
Your little brother is clumsy, and the soda he
spills stains your jacket. We all have faults,
and these are faults you need to forgive.
Forgiving someone—letting them off
the hook—often has to be an act of will. If
you wait till you *feel* like forgiving someone,

you may never do it. And we are commanded to forgive. God would not command us to do something if it were impossible to do. Forgiveness is real the moment we choose to forgive, but it can take weeks or months for our feelings to change, depending on how big the hurt is.

True forgiveness can make a positive impact on the forgiven person. Without it, bitterness and hurt feelings grow even stronger. Forgiving another person does not mean you're saying what they did was okay. But it DOES mean that you are giving up your right to revenge, or paying them back. Revenge and hatred may hurt others, but they are more likely to destroy *you*.

Be patient, and cultivate the forgiving habit. Then watch the peace and joy grow in your own heart.

Did You Know ...

that we are to build up our neighbors and please them? It's all a part of dealing with one another's weaknesses. Read Romans 15:1–2.

More To Explore: Ephesians 4:2–3

Girl Talk:

Is there someone you need to forgive? Are you willing to give up revenge toward them? Are you ready to move on?

God Talk:

"Lord, it's really hard, but I choose to forgive _____. I don't want to be bitter anymore. Please help me to really forgive them and get on with my life. Thank you for your willingness to always forgive me. Amen."

Devotion #25

"I pray that out of his glorious riches he may
strengthen you with power through his
Spirit in your inner being, so that Christ may
dwell in your hearts through faith."
—Ephesians 3:16–17 (NIV)

Strength from Within

Others often disappoint us, and we also disappoint God.
At other times we're sick or we're just plain tired. We wonder
if we can go on. Maybe not—in our *own* strength. But God has
an unlimited supply of strength available to those who have
trusted in Christ.

Kylie ate a whole box of cookies, after promising herself
she'd eat just two. She was so tired of trying to lose the
weight her doctor suggested. Amber was disappointed
too, but in her mom. She'd promised *again* to make
it to her soccer game, but when Amber scored
the winning goal, her mom wasn't there to
see it—*again*. Amber felt like quitting.

What can these girls do for strength
when their own has run out? As believers, they can pray for help. "In the day
when I cried out, You answered me, and

made me bold with strength in my soul" (Psalm 138:3 NKJV).

Whenever we experience a disappointment, we need to be refreshed and encouraged. As you trust in God more and more, Jesus will be more and more "at home" in your heart. When that happens, your disappointments won't seem like such a big deal because you'll know you're not alone. Even more than God wants to remove your pain or uncomfortable circumstances, he wants to use them first to help you grow.

Instead of focusing on negative circumstances on the outside, pray for God to strengthen you on the inside. He will!

Did You Know ...

that even though our bodies wear out more each day, our souls are being renewed daily? In 2 Corinthians 4:16–18, Paul wrote that our faith is keeping our soul new every day, whether our body works or not. Read these verses for great encouragement!

More To Explore: Philippians 4:19 and Isaiah 40:29–31

Girl Talk:

Think about the last time you were disappointed. Did you dwell on how bad things were for you? Did you ask God for help and encouragement?

God Talk:

"Lord, sometimes I feel too weak to keep going every day. Please help me to remember that you will give me all the strength I need. Thank you for always being here for me. Amen."

Devotion #26

"Do you not know that in a race all the runners run, but only one gets the prize? Run in such a way as to get the prize." —1 Corinthians 9:24 (NIV)

Running for Your Life

Believers are like runners in a race. In order to finish well, runners have to focus on the finish line. Heaven is the finish line for believers. If you want to live a life that counts, that has purpose, you need to live today while keeping the future in mind at all times.

June had accepted Christ as her Savior two summers before at church camp. For more than a year, she read her Bible daily, talked to her friends about Jesus, faithfully attended Sunday school, and was careful to choose godly friends. When she went to middle school in sixth grade, things changed. She got busy with new friends, ball games, movies, and shopping. She wasn't doing anything wrong—yet— but she had lost her focus. She stopped reading her Bible and praying. She dropped the most important things from her life in exchange for temporary fun. She stopped growing spiritually.

In our daily living, we must keep our purpose clearly in mind. We are living for eternity, not for our lives here on earth. It's easy to forget that. We get so busy—and so comfortable. We become lazy and too concerned with our immediate happiness. That makes it easier to slip into an ungodly lifestyle. We must remember that like the racers in training, we haven't arrived yet either. This life is our training ground and our race.

To be sure that you finish the race with strength, do what the athletes do. Set goals for your spiritual growth, write them down, and keep track of the progress you make. Know that progress takes time, but keep at it.

Keep your eyes on Jesus, and go for the gold!

Did You Know ...

that the prize at the end of our earthly race is a crown of righteousness? This means the Lord will honor those who complete his will for their lives. Timothy talks about winning his race and receiving the prize from Jesus. Read 2 Timothy 4:7–8.

More To Explore: Hebrews 12:1 and Philippians 3:14

Girl Talk:

Do you get caught up in what's cool, what's fun? How well do you keep your focus on God and what he has to teach you?

God Talk:

"Lord, I don't always remember that being a Christian is a choice that I need to keep making. Please help me remember that I *always* need to focus on you, not just some of the time. I want to put you first! Thank you. Amen."

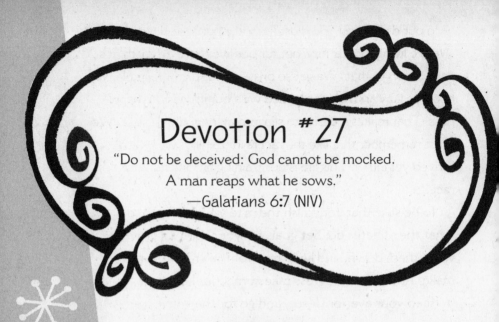

Devotion #27

"Do not be deceived: God cannot be mocked.
A man reaps what he sows."
—Galatians 6:7 (NIV)

A Bounty of Blessings

Don't be misled. Remember that you can't ignore God's laws and get away with it. You always harvest *what* you plant. (You plant corn—you harvest corn.) You always harvest *more* than you plant or sow. (You plant a bushel of corn, and you reap hundreds of bushels back.) You always harvest *later* than you sow. (You plant corn, you wait during the growing season, and you reap during the harvest season.) The same is true of your actions—your seeds—no matter what kind.

You always get the kind of harvest that matches your seed. A farmer plants corn expecting a harvest of corn—not carrots. Your harvest will also match the seed you sow. Galatians 6:8 (NIV) says, "The one who sows to please his sinful nature, from that nature will reap destruction; the one who sows to please the Spirit, from the Spirit will reap eternal life."

So this principle works both positively and negatively. Those determined to do whatever they please, no matter what God's Word says, can count on reaping a negative harvest of problems and destruction. For those living a godly lifestyle, it is a promise of reward and blessings, and an encouragement to persist in doing what's right.

What kinds of things can you sow as seed? Money you give away can be a seed you plant, but anything you do for someone else's good is a seed you sow. It might be a smile, an encouraging word, making time to listen, praying for someone, doing a favor for your mom—it's all good seed to plant when done from an unselfish heart with unselfish motives.

Your future lies in the generous seeds you plant today.

Did You Know ...

that Paul spells out very clearly what will happen to us, depending on what we decide to sow? We will get either eternal life for doing good, or trouble and distress for doing evil. Read Romans 2:6–10.

More To Explore: 1 Corinthians 9:6 and Hosea 10:12–13

Girl Talk:

Think about the past day or two. What do you think you've been sowing? Were you encouraging and helpful? Or were you sulking and backstabbing?

God Talk:

"Lord, I don't always remember that everything I do makes a difference. I want to plant the right seeds for those around me. Please help me to rely on you and to do the right thing in everything I do. Amen."

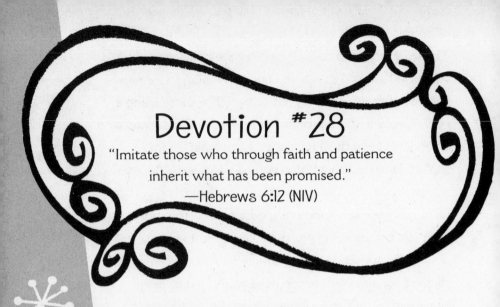

Devotion #28

"Imitate those who through faith and patience
inherit what has been promised."
—Hebrews 6:12 (NIV)

Promise To Be Patient

The Bible is full of promises for the believer,
promises for peace, success, joy, love, friendship,
rewarding work, and much more. It takes two things for
these promises to come true. The first ingredient is faith:
believing God's Word is true. The second necessary ingredient is patience: keeping a positive attitude while you wait.
Many believers have faith; few have patience. You need both.
"After he had *patiently endured*, he obtained the promise"
(Hebrews 6:15 NKJV, emphasis added).

Jillian's best friend was moving away. They'd been best
friends and next-door neighbors for five years, and Jillian
was brokenhearted at the news. She claimed Psalm
147:3: "[God] heals the heartbroken and ban-
dages their wounds" (MSG). She truly
believed God would do that for her, but
when a week went by and she still felt
sad, she decided the promise didn't work.
Jillian was wrong. The promise is sure,
and God's Word can be counted on. Jillian

had faith—but she was missing the ingredient of patience.

Patience is the ability to stay steady during the challenging storms of life. You usually have to wait a length of time before you receive your promise. It's like planting a seed (your faith), then waiting for the harvest to appear. The waiting time is the testing time. Will we continue to believe God for the promise when things get tough? Will we trust that God is bringing his promises to pass even before we see the results? "Without wavering, let us hold tightly to the hope we say we have, for God can be trusted to keep his promise" (Hebrews 10:23 NLT).

Are you waiting for a promise of God in your life? Then practice both faith and patience. It's a winning combination.

Did You Know ...

that you will get what God has promised only if you refuse to quit? You need to keep living the life God wants you to, as long as he needs you to. Read Hebrews 10:36.

More To Explore: Luke 8:15 and Romans 2:7

Girl Talk:

How's your patience level? Can you stick things out, or do you want things done right away? The next time something seems to take too long, talk to God and ask him to strengthen you.

God Talk:

"Lord, it's so hard to be patient. I really do want to wait for your perfect timing. Please help me stay calm and know you are taking care of everything. Thank you for all you do for me. Amen."

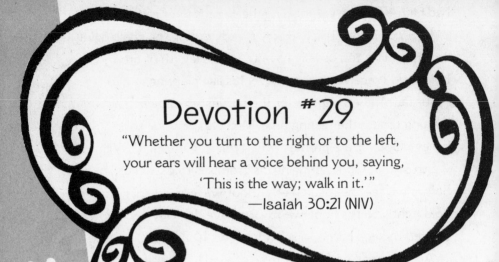

Devotion #29

"Whether you turn to the right or to the left,
your ears will hear a voice behind you, saying,
'This is the way; walk in it.'"
—Isaiah 30:21 (NIV)

Following The Paths of Righteousness

God promises to lead us and guide us when we
don't know what to do. As believers, we have the Holy
Spirit living inside us. He is always there to help us find the
right path. If we are truly listening, we'll hear that "still small
voice" inside giving us sure directions.

Jill doesn't know what to do. She just found out that her
friend Merissa copied her math homework and turned it in as
her own. Jill knows cheating is wrong, but she doesn't want
to make her friend mad. What's the right thing to do? Kyla
has permission to sign up for one activity in the summer, but she loves both swimming and softball.
Which one should she choose?

We all need to make decisions—big and
little—many times each day. How do we
know the right choices to make? The
title is your relationship with God. The
closer you are to him, the easier you will
hear his voice and direction.

Being close to God means learning what he likes and dislikes through reading his Word. Hearing God clearly requires that we give up what *we* want and are willing to do what *he* wants. Hearing from God often takes time, so it calls for patience and continuing to pray. If you're willing to do these things consistently, you'll find it much easier to hear God's voice when you need guidance.

Remember, God knows everything about your situation, even though it looks confusing to you. And he says, "I will lead the blind by ways they have not known, along unfamiliar paths I will guide them; I will turn the darkness into light before them and make the rough places smooth" (Isaiah 42:16 NIV).

When you need direction, go to God. He is a sure and trustworthy guide.

Did You Know ...

that God will supply all your needs, "like a spring whose waters never fail"? Keep trusting in the Lord, and your waters will keep flowing! Read Isaiah 58:11.

More To Explore: Psalms 143:8; 32:8; and Proverbs 3:5–6

Girl Talk:

Do you have times when you just don't know what to do? Who do you turn to first? Is it God? Your mom? Your friend?

God Talk:

"Lord, I have times when I don't know what to do. Please guide me and show me what to do. You want what is best for me, and I thank you so much for that! Amen."

Devotion #30

"If we love our Christian brothers and sisters, it
proves that we have passed from death to eternal life.
But a person who has no love is still dead."
—1 John 3:14 (NLT)

Let Them Know You by Your Love

If our lives have been changed, we'll prove it by
the love we show toward others. When we fail to act in
love, we are still walking in darkness. Jesus told his closest
followers, "By this all will know that you are My disciples, if
you have love for one another" (John 13:35 NKJV).

Jenna and Samantha were in the same bunkhouse at
church camp. They were both slender, tanned, pretty, well
dressed, and "cool." They refused to mingle with the other
three girls in their bunkhouse, secretly calling them
"losers." Although Jenna and Samantha sang the praise
songs, they weren't walking in love toward others.
They walked in spiritual darkness.

The proof that you're a believer is in how
you treat others. Yes, we all get hurt and
offended sometimes. We're all imperfect
human beings trying to live together.
But are you truly making an effort to
love others? Do you forgive people and

show them concern and respect? Or do you fake being a Christian? When someone offends you, are you outwardly "nice," but hold a grudge and avoid that person forever? "Dear children, let us stop just saying we love each other; let us really show it by our actions" (1 John 3:18 NLT).

If we're not trying hard to grow and walk in loving relationship with the people around us—at home, at school, at church—we're just proving that God hasn't touched our lives. Jesus said people would know his disciples by their love for one another (see John 13:35). If people were to judge you by the love you show to others, what would they believe about you?

Grow daily in the expressions of your love toward others—and see what joy fills your heart!

Did You Know ...

that if you don't love your brother (or neighbor), you cannot love God? First John 4:20 says if we can't even love what we see, then we can't love what we *don't* see.

God Talk:

"Lord, please help me to be loving, on both the outside and inside. I want to be a great example of your love. Thank you! Amen."

More To Explore: 1 Thessalonians 4:9–10 and 1 John 2:9, 11

Girl Talk:

When you interact with others, do you put on a phony front, or does the condition of your heart match your words? When God looks at your heart, what does he see?

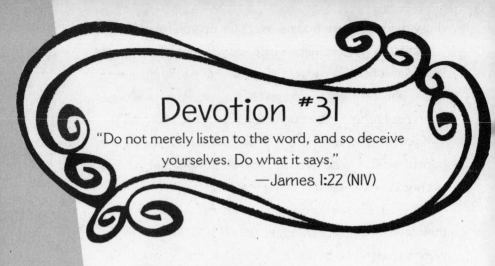

"Do not merely listen to the word, and so deceive
yourselves. Do what it says."
—James 1:22 (NIV)

Don't Fool Yourself

It's great to read the Bible and hear it preached
and pay attention to it. But don't stop there! Practice
what it says. Carry out its directions. If you don't, you
are only fooling yourself into thinking you're a follower of
Christ.

When bad things happen, we often pray more and
eagerly search our Bibles for answers. That's exactly the right
thing to do, but we might not like what we find. The bully on
the bus who trips you? The Word says you are to pray for
those who persecute you and pick on you, but not take
revenge. How about the classmate who makes nasty
remarks or teases you with unkind names? It hurts a lot.
The Bible says we are to speak the truth IN LOVE
to this person, not call her names back. Don't
fool yourself into thinking that you're behaving like a Christian just by reading the
Bible. You must also do what it says.
Pray for that bully. Deal with that nasty
classmate, but use kind words.
Don't be someone God says this about:

"I called you so often, but you didn't come. I reached out to you, but you paid no attention. You ignored my advice and rejected the correction I offered" (Proverbs 1:24–25 NLT). Instead, be determined to put into practice what you read. You won't do it perfectly, and that's okay. But as best you can, carry out what you believe God is telling you to do in a situation.

The Word is powerful. Put it into practice, and see what marvelous changes God makes in your life.

Did You Know ...

that Jesus compared our faith to the foundation of a house? If the foundation is built on rock, it will stand through storms. If it is built on sand, it will fall when storms come. Can your faith stand up through problems and conflicts in your life? Read Luke 6:46–49.

Girl Talk:

When faced with a tough situation, do you turn to God? Do you read the Bible and do what it says?

More To Explore: Matthew 7:21 and James 2:14–20

God Talk:

"Lord, thank you for giving me your Word. Help me to read it and obey, instead of what I want to do. Thank you for giving me guidance. Amen."

Mini-Quiz:

Just believing that there is a God isn't enough. What surprising group also believes there is a God?

demons (James 2:19 NKJV)

Devotion #32

"If you fully obey the LORD your God and carefully
follow all his commands I give you today . . . All these
blessings will come upon you and accompany
you if you obey the LORD your God."
—Deuteronomy 28:1–2 (NIV)

The Blessings of Obedience

All people want to be full of peace and joy, having all their
needs met. God tells you how that can happen. It's really quite
simple. If you want to be blessed, be careful to follow God's
commands and fully obey them. If you will do this, God's blessings of protection and abundance will attach themselves to you!
Do you want to have a trimmer, healthier body? If you
show self-control (a fruit of the Spirit) in your eating and
exercise habits, you will be blessed with that healthy
body. Do you want to have a new CD player or a
new outfit? Then handle your money and
your job opportunities according to God's
principles (like working hard and finish-
ing what you start). Do you want the
blessing of deep friendships? Then be
obedient to commands like thinking of
others' interests as well as your own, and

not gossiping, since backbiting separates friends.

We must be willing to do what God says to do if we want to experience what God has promised. He has given us guidelines for living a happy, blessed life, but it's up to each of us to follow those guidelines. In many, many cases, we are responsible for the outcome of our future. Although God wants to bless all of us, many of us cut off our own blessings by disobedience in some area. Jesus said, "Blessed are those who hear the word of God and keep it!" (Luke 11:28 NKJV).

Want a super-blessed life? Then dig into the Word of God and start obeying your way to blessings!

Did You Know ...

that God made it simple for the Israelites to obey him after they left Egypt? He spelled it all out to Moses on Mount Sinai, describing what would happen if they were obedient or disobedient. Read Leviticus 26:3–46 to get all the details.

More To Explore: Exodus 15:26 and Isaiah 1:18–20

Girl Talk:

Do you have needs or wants that have not been fulfilled yet? Are they things you want, or what God wants? (Or both?)

God Talk:

"Lord, there are always lots of things I want, but I know that you might want different things for me. Help me to read the Bible every day and keep praying, to find out what you want me to do. Your will be done! Amen."

Devotion #33

"Our purpose is to please God, not people. He is
the one who examines the motives of our hearts.
Never once did we try to win you with flattery,
as you very well know. And God is our witness that
we were not just pretending to be your friends
so you would give us money!"
—1 Thessalonians 2:4–5 (NLT)

Honor Your Friendships

The reason for your actions should be to please God, not people. God tests and knows the purposes hidden in your heart, the reasons for how you treat your friends. Do not try to win friends with false flattery. And don't pretend to be friends with someone because she can give you things. When someone who rarely speaks to you suddenly gushes with praise about your "ultracool outfit" or your "brilliant science project" or "your totally fabulous hair," don't you smell something fishy? Most of us have a good nose for false praise and flattery. Our first thought is: *Okay, what do you want from me?* Have you caught *yourself* doing the same thing with friends sometimes? Do you give honest praise? Or do you flatter someone so she'll invite you to her pizza party, let you borrow her cool sweater, or give you a ride to the game?

Paul says in this verse that personal profit was never his aim in treating his friends well: "nor did we put on a mask to cover up greed" (1 Thessalonians 2:5 NIV). Don't wear a phony mask with your friends. Don't try to hide the reasons for things you say and do. Be honest with your praise, but watch your reasons for it. Do it out of love, not to get something in return. If you're not sure of your reasons, use this as your test: Will these words and actions please God, or just people?

Please God first in your friendships—and you'll be a true friend!

Did You Know ...

that Paul came without lofty ideas when he first met with the church in Corinth? He spoke very simply. He wanted God's Word to be the focus, not him! Read 1 Corinthians 2:1–5.

More To Explore: James 4:4

Girl Talk:

Look at your friendships. Are you friends because you honestly like them or because of what they can give you? How would God see your friendships?

God Talk:

"Lord, I sometimes think too selfishly. Help me to be honest with everyone I meet, including you. Thank you for your loving care. Amen."

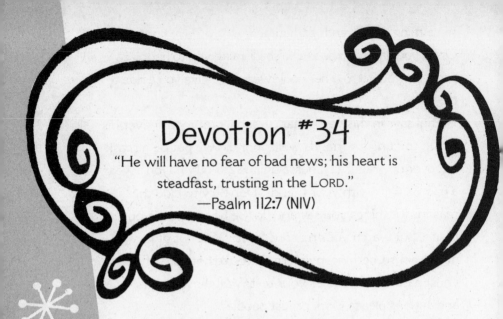

Devotion #34

"He will have no fear of bad news; his heart is
steadfast, trusting in the LORD."
—Psalm 112:7 (NIV)

Unshakable Trust

Some people have no anxiety about coming danger
or receiving bad news. Their minds and emotions are
steady, firm, unwavering, and unshakable. How do they
attain this wonderful state of being? By trusting in the Lord,
relying on him, putting their faith in him, and obeying his
commands.

We all receive bad news sometimes. That's part of life. It
might be fairly minor, like your friend can't go to the movie
with you after all. It might be more serious, like getting an
F on a test or your report card. Or the bad news can be
extremely painful, like the death of a favorite
grandparent or your parents' divorce. We find
it very easy to get upset at bad news, cry-
ing and screaming and lashing out at
people, or becoming severely depressed.
Instead, we are to have a calm, "steadfast heart" that trusts in the Lord.

A heart with unshakable faith is needed

so we can stop, pray for wisdom, and sit back and allow God to work. God will handle those problems that we don't have the ability to control. Things change constantly, and some of those changes bring bad news. But God never changes. His love is unchanging and everlasting. He can (if we let him) work even bad things out for our good (Romans 8:28). Always remember that the bad news you receive does NOT take God by surprise. He knows when it is coming, and he's ready to help you get through it calmly, so that you come out on the other side even stronger.

Trust in God, no matter what kind of news you receive. He'll never let you down!

Did You Know ...

that before David was king, he was pursued by King Saul's army? Saul wanted David dead, but David knew God would take care of him. Read Psalm 27:1–3.

More To Explore: Romans 8:28 and John 14:1

Girl Talk:

When you get bad news, how do you feel? What do you usually do? Do you pray to God about it?

God Talk:

"Lord, when bad things happen, I am not usually calm. Please help me stay calm and have firm faith in you. Thank you for never leaving my side. Amen."

Beauty 101:

To help stay cool on the outside when under pressure, use an antiperspirant. To stay cool *inside*, take ten slow, deep breaths. This gives you time to calm down, instead of having an ugly temper tantrum!

Devotion #35

"Caleb silenced the people before Moses and said,
'We should go up and take possession of the land,
for we can certainly do it.' But the men who had
gone up with him said, 'We can't attack those
people; they are stronger than we are.'"
—Numbers 13:30–31 (NIV)

The "Truth" Shall Set You Free

After wandering in the wilderness for forty years, the
Israelites finally arrived at the Promised Land. Twelve men were
sent as spies into the land, to bring back a report. Only two
men, Joshua and Caleb, had a positive report. They believed
God and encouraged the people to take possession of the
Promised Land. But the other ten spies were afraid, and
they discouraged the people from trying. They ignored
the truth of God's power, looked at the "facts"
(their own small strength), and decided they
couldn't conquer the cities there.

Do you ever do that? Do you spend
time telling God or other people how big
your problems are and how small your
strength is to overcome them? Do you
say, "I just can't go on. I can't take this anymore"? Or do you speak God's truth, which

says, "I can do everything through him who gives me strength" (Philippians 4:13 NIV)? When you have a fight with your best friend or your parents, do you listen to your emotions and wail, "Nobody loves me!" Or do you repeat Jesus' words from John 15:9 (NLT), which says, "I have loved you even as the Father has loved me. Remain in my love"?

Use your mouth for the purpose God created it. Choose to believe and speak God's truth, not your fears. Don't be like the Israelite spies who stared at the "facts" and forgot about God's power. Those unbelieving men were never allowed to enter the Promised Land.

There may be some unpleasant "facts" in your life right now, but get into the Word of God. Find out God's *truth* on the matter. Then choose to speak God's truth!

Did You Know ...

that in Isaiah 41:10–16, God tells us we can crush mountains because he is with us? He repeats "Do not fear" more than once. This is a great passage of reassurance!

Girl Talk:

Do you ever make problems bigger than they really are? Do you ever ask God for peace about your problems?

More To Explore: Numbers 14:6–9, 24

God Talk:

"Lord, I know I complain about my problems sometimes. I guess I want sympathy from other people. Please help me remember that you already know about my problems and that you will get me through them. Thank you! Amen."

Devotion #36

"Stay away from the love of money; be satisfied with what you have. For God has said, 'I will never fail you. I will never forsake you.'"
—Hebrews 13:5 (NLT)

Fighting Discontent

Keep your life free from envy, wishing you had money or things that belong to someone else. Be content with the things you have. You don't need to be afraid. God will provide for your needs. He is totally dependable, and he'll never leave you in the lurch. You can count on him! Kelsey was content with her clothes and bedroom until she visited Britney, who had a walk-in closet full of outfits and an entertainment center in her bedroom. Rosa liked the home-made curtains and decorations in her room till she hung out in the mall and saw the things she could have if only she had more money. Both girls came home dissatisfied, wishing they had what they'd seen that day. Suddenly their own clothes and homes seemed shabby and outdated and totally uncool. Instead of trusting God to meet their needs, both girls had fallen into a big trap: envy.

Has envy over someone else's posses-sions ever gripped you? You can be free if you want to regain your contentment. First, if you always come home depressed from the mall or your rich friend's house, then limit your time spent there. Invite friends to your home instead, providing fun activities instead of fancy furnishings. Also, be thankful. Thank God daily for the blessings in your life, for the roof over your head, for your bed and clothes and food. The more you thank God for never failing you, the more content you will grow with the things you already have.

If there's something you truly need, God will provide. In the meantime, be satisfied!

Did You Know ...

that in the days of Joshua, a man and his family were stoned for taking things that didn't belong to them? God had commanded the Israelites not to take things from the people they conquered, but Achan did anyway. Read Joshua 7.

GirL TaLk:

When was the last time you felt envious of someone? Does it eat at you? Ask God to help you be content with what you have.

More To Explore: Luke 8:14 and Matthew 6:25

God TaLk:

"Lord, right now, I feel envious of _____. Please take that feeling away. I want to be content with what I have. Thank you for providing all I really need. Amen."

Devotion #37

"Do not be afraid, for I have ransomed you. I have called you by name; you are mine. When you go through deep waters and great trouble, I will be with you. When you go through rivers of difficulty, you will not drown! When you walk through the fire of oppression, you will not be burned up; the flames will not consume you. For I am the LORD, your God, the Holy One of Israel, your Savior."
—Isaiah 43:1-3 (NLT)

A Friend in Times of Trouble

If you have accepted Jesus as your Savior, you don't need to be afraid anymore. God has saved and reclaimed you. Now you belong to him. Even when troubles seem too big to survive, God will walk you through them. You won't drown in your difficulty. You won't be destroyed, no matter how hard it gets sometimes.

Even when you forget to pray, God never leaves you. When you fail in your tests and trials, he never leaves you. Although you may not feel God's presence, he never leaves you. Life can sometimes hand us some very deep rivers of trouble. You may be adjusting to a new stepfamily. Your health may be in serious danger. You may have a family member fighting in the military. You may live in a city where serious crime happens daily. Is God still there, walking beside you? YES!

If you can't feel God's presence, pray. Often. The more you talk to God, the more closely you will feel him nearby. Then you will be able to say, like the apostle Paul, "The Lord stood at my side and gave me strength . . . The Lord will rescue me from every evil attack and will bring me safely to his heavenly kingdom" (2 Timothy 4:17–18 NIV).

God walks beside you daily, to encourage, protect, and comfort you. You belong to him!

Did You Know . . .

that Daniel's friends, who were loyal to God, survived being thrown into a roaring furnace? Read about them in Daniel 3:8–27.

More To Explore: Exodus 33:17

Girl Talk:

Do you ever feel alone when things aren't going right? Have you talked to God about what's happening?

God Talk:

"Lord, you know what I'm going through. Please give me your peace and hope. I need your help to get through this. Thank you. Amen."

Mini-Quiz:

_____ prayed, "O that you would bless me and enlarge my territory." God granted his request.

(a) David   (c) Ahab

(b) Jabez   (d) Joseph

Jabez

Devotion #38

"Do not make friends with a hot-tempered man, do not associate with one easily angered, or you may learn his ways and get yourself ensnared."
—Proverbs 22:24–25 (NIV)

The Influence of Anger

Keep away from angry, short-tempered people. Don't make friends with them, or you will learn to be like them. This sets a snare—or a trap—for your soul.

Tamara is new at school, and two girls have been friendly to her. One girl snarls to get her own way and has a tongue sharp enough to slice people in two. The second girl is quiet when she's upset, nursing her anger and refusing to talk with people. Which girl should she choose for a friend? Actually, neither. One is obviously a hothead, and she's easy to spot. But the girl who is easily offended, holds a grudge, and gives people the silent treatment is also an angry girl. Different personalities show anger in different ways.

Hot-tempered people can be strangely attractive. They seem to have a lot of power. No one tells them what to do. They don't put up with anything they don't like. People give in to them to keep the peace. That's what a snare is: something that looks attractive, but it's fooling you. It's like beautiful bait on a fishhook—and once you bite, you're caught. Hanging around with angry people, seeing how they handle their lives and problems, can teach you to be just like them. The Bible says these are the characteristics of a hot-tempered man: he's reckless and does foolish things (Proverbs 14:16–17), stirs up disagreements and strife (Proverbs 15:18), and commits many sins (Proverbs 29:22). Is this the kind of behavior you hope to learn? Then don't make friends with an angry, hotheaded person.

Be slow to anger, and choose your friends wisely.

Did You Know ...

that acting like an angry, hot-tempered person is a snare for your soul? A hothead makes foolish decisions because she has no self-control! And "a person without self-control is as defenseless as a city with broken-down walls" (Proverbs 25:28 NLT).

More To Explore: Proverbs 14:29; 19:19

Girl Talk:

Are you easily offended? Do you ever shoot off your mouth with-out thinking? Do you know someone who does? How do you think God feels about that?

God Talk:

"Lord, sometimes I lose my cool and spout off with my mouth. Please help me to stay calm when I get angry. I want to show others your example. Thank you! Amen."

Devotion #39

"If you forgive men when they sin against you, your heavenly Father will also forgive you. But if you do not forgive men their sins, your Father will not forgive your sins." —Matthew 6:14–15 (NIV)

Forgive or Be Forgotten

People hurt us or do wrong things to us, sometimes accidentally, and sometimes on purpose. Either way, we need to forgive them if we expect God to forgive the wrongs we do. But if we refuse to forgive others, God will not forgive our sins either.

Serena got along well with everyone at school—except Timothy. He tormented her every chance he got, with name-calling, tripping her, and swiping her homework. She had no idea why she was his target. Serena went to church, read her Bible, and prayed regularly. She forgave everyone who hurt her—except Timothy. His treatment was so totally unfair that she was sure God would understand. But God doesn't make exceptions to the forgiveness rule.

We want God to forgive us for the wrongs we have done. And he will, unless . . .

Unless we refuse to forgive someone for a wrong they did to us. In that case, God won't forgive you either. That's a pretty strong statement!

Part of the Lord's Prayer says, "Forgive us our debts, as we forgive our debtors" (Matthew 6:12 NKJV). This means we are asking God to forgive us *in the same way* we forgive others. If we hold a grudge and refuse to forgive, neither will God forgive us. If we freely forgive, we'll be forgiven.

So start your day with a clean conscience: totally forgiven.

Did You Know ...

that the parable of the unmerciful servant is a great example of forgiving if you expect to be forgiven? Read Matthew 18:21–35.

More To Explore: Mark 11:25–26

Girl Talk:

Do you need to forgive someone? Are bitter feelings coming between you and God's forgiveness?

God Talk:

"Lord, if there is anyone I need to forgive, please help me know. I want to be right with you. Please help me to forgive them and let go of past bitterness. Thank you. Amen."

Devotion #40

"I call to God, and the LORD saves me. Evening, morning and noon I cry out in distress, and he hears my voice."—Psalm 55:16–17 (NIV)

God Is Always There

No matter what time it is—morning, noon, or night—God is never too busy to listen when you call on him. When you have troubles—regardless of the kind or how serious they are—God hears and answers. The Lord rescues!

When Lauren woke up and rolled over, the pain in her shoulder reminded her of her bike accident and broken collarbone. "God, I know I shouldn't complain," she whispered, "but I really hate wearing this brace! It's ugly, and I can't run now, and it hurts worse than the doctor said it would. Help me!" Did God hear her cry? Absolutely. When Lauren lay quietly, other things came to her mind: how lucky she was not to be killed when the car hit her, how blessed she was with a mom who helped her dress, how lucky she was to have friends who carried her books, and how fortunate she was to live in a country where doctors were available to set bones. By the time she was done praying—which is both talking *and* listening to God—Lauren's feelings were the opposite.

We can trust that God hears us when we cry out to him. We can trust him to handle the concerns we face each day, and to identify every worry and care that troubles us. By giving up "ownership" of our worries, we transfer the problem to God to solve. "Give all your worries and cares to God, for he cares about what happens to you" (1 Peter 5:7 NLT). Handing over our cares to God requires faith: we trust God will support us as he has promised.

If you need help—any time of the day or night—call on God. You'll never get a busy signal, and he's got all the time in the world to listen to you.

Did You Know ...

that even if God hasn't answered right away, he still bears your burden? When you think about what's troubling you, thank him for carrying that burden for you. Read Psalm 68:19.

Girl Talk:

When you have troubles, do you dwell on them? Or do you count your blessings? Do you talk to God about your troubles?

More To Explore: Psalm 5:2–3 and Micah 7:7

God Talk:

"Lord, I know things won't be perfect for me. When I am in pain or have problems, help me to come to you and give you my fears. Thank you for everything you give me daily. Amen."

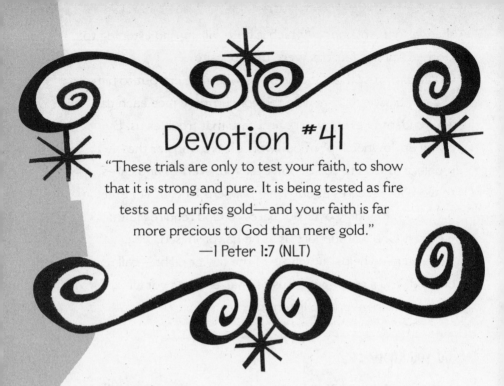

Devotion #41

"These trials are only to test your faith, to show
that it is strong and pure. It is being tested as fire
tests and purifies gold—and your faith is far
more precious to God than mere gold."
—1 Peter 1:7 (NLT)

Tested by Fire

The problems you run into are common to all believers.
These difficult times test your faith, to show that it is strong.
Going through tests successfully also helps get rid of your
faults and defects. It's like fire that purifies gold and brings its
impurities to the surface. Your faith in God is being tested as
fire tests gold—and your faith is worth far more to God
than mere gold.

Storms of life *will* come. Jesus has promised to
be with us WHEN we walk through fiery trials
and tests, not IF we go through tests. He's
with us, alongside us, to encourage us not
to faint or give up. A test in life is like a
test at school: you either pass or fail. If
you look at your math test, try a couple of
problems, and then quit because it's too
hard, you'll fail the test. Fail enough tests, and

you'll have to repeat that class or grade. On the other hand, studying and preparing yourself will help you pass the test.

The same applies to the tests you'll encounter in life, whether they are health tests, friendship tests, schoolwork tests, or family tests. If you quit when things get hard, you'll fail the test. God will forgive you, he'll pick you up and dust you off—but you'll have to repeat the test. Studying for the tests of life—reading and thinking deeply about what God's Word says to do—will help you pass your tests and come out much stronger.

Be determined to come through your tests strong and pure—more precious than gold.

Did You Know ...

that we go through trials for the same reason gold is heated up—to get rid of unwanted bits and pieces that are in us? Read Isaiah 48:10; Zechariah 13:9; and Proverbs 17:3.

More To Explore: 1 Peter 4:12–13 and Job 23:10–12

Girl Talk:

When you have a test at school, how hard do you study? Do you think you are as well prepared for trials that life will send you?

God Talk:

"Lord, I know there will be trials in my life. Please help me to be prepared for them. I want to read the Bible more and talk with you. Thank you for never leaving me. Amen."

Fun Factoid:

Gold reaches 2,100 degrees Fahrenheit when being purified!

Devotion #42

"Everyone who competes in the games goes into strict training. They do it to get a crown that will not last; but we do it to get a crown that will last forever."
—1 Corinthians 9:25 (NIV)

The Price of The Prize

The Greeks had games similar to our summer Olympics. Athletes who competed were in very strict training for months before. They had to develop strict self-control in their eating, drinking, rest times, and their physical workouts. They did all that to win a prize that wouldn't last. The prize was a crown—not a royal crown, but a wreath or circular band made of leaves and flowers. Believers are training to win a crown that lasts forever.

Bobbi was in gymnastics. She practiced two hours a day, got up early on Saturdays for private lessons, and turned down sweets to keep in top form. She intended to win a medal at the competition. Lindsay read her Bible and prayed before bedtime, got up early on Sunday to make it to Sunday school. She skipped PG–13 and R-rated movies, even though she was ridiculed for it. She wanted to win a prize too. Bobbi's medal would rust. Lindsay's prize would last forever.

Strict training for athletes sometimes includes muscle cramps, sports injuries, and accidents. But to win the game, sportsmen are willing to endure pain. Sadly, few Christians are willing to endure pain in order to grow in their spiritual lives. They concentrate too much on the pain and not enough on the reward that's coming. Believers can learn much from dedicated athletes. We too need to focus on the prize, a crown that will last for eternity. Your focus will determine your attitude about whatever pain or hardships you encounter.

Keep your eye on the prize!

Did You Know ...

that Paul makes several references to athletes in his letters to Timothy? One or both of them probably enjoyed sports. Who knew we might have sports fans in the Bible? Read 1 Timothy 6:12 and 2 Timothy 2:5 to hear more.

More To Explore: James 1:12 and 1 Peter 1:3–4

Girl Talk:

Do you enjoy any sports or hobbies? How hard do you work at them? How hard do you work to improve your quiet time with God?

God Talk:

"Lord, I make time for some activities, but I seem to run out when learning about you. Please help me to remember to use my energy for you first. I want to know more about you. Thank you. Amen."

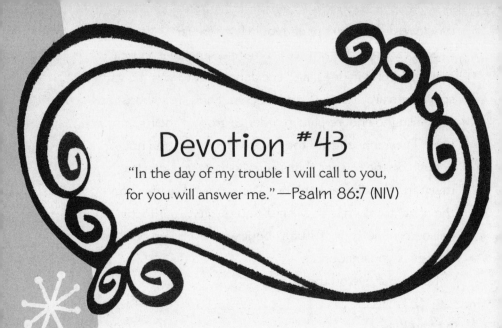

Devotion #43

"In the day of my trouble I will call to you,
for you will answer me."—Psalm 86:7 (NIV)

A Direct Line To God

When we spot trouble—crimes, fires, car
accidents—we call 911 for emergency help. We are confident when we dial 911 that the call will be answered. Help
is on its way. In the same manner, you have a hotline to
heaven. God's phone line is never busy, you never get put on
hold, and you never get his voice mail. He has a cell phone
plan where you get free minutes, twenty-four hours a day,
seven days a week. You can talk to God any time—day or
night. And his answers are always available in his Word.

Rosa took a wrong turn on the way home, and
suddenly she was biking through a creepy
neighborhood she didn't recognize. She was
scared! Lyndsey went to pay for her
hamburger and discovered her purse
was empty. What should she do? Anna
came home from vacation to find that
her best friend had a *new* best friend.
Who could Anna talk to?

They all need to dial God for help. If YOU need help, try these "Emergency Numbers":

- When you're in danger, call Psalm 91.
- When God seems far away, call Psalm 139.
- When you're lonely and fearful, call Psalm 23.
- When you need peace and rest, call Matthew 11:28–30.
- When you need courage for a task, call Joshua 1.
- If you're depressed, call Psalm 27.
- If your wallet and piggy bank are empty, call Psalm 37.
- When feeling sadness or sorrow, call John 14.
- When you need forgiveness, call Psalm 51.
- If you're worried, call Matthew 6:25–34.

We all need help sometimes. You can always pray, and you can go to God's Word. God promises to meet your needs. So give God a call!

Did You Know ...

that David praised God for the way he was created? "I praise you because I am fearfully and wonderfully made" (see Psalm 139:13–14 NIV). God did so much just to make you! You can trust him with anything!

Girl Talk:

Now that you know you can talk to God about anything, who can help you find answers in the Bible? Who can support you as you work on getting closer to God?

More To Explore: Philippians 4:19

God Talk:

"Lord, thank you for the Bible and for loved ones who can help me. Thank you for always being there for me. I love you! Amen."

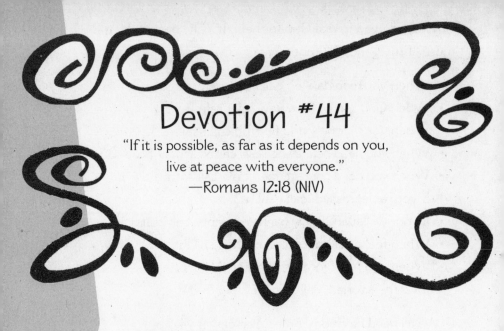

Devotion #44

"If it is possible, as far as it depends on you,
live at peace with everyone."
—Romans 12:18 (NIV)

Living in Peace

Do your part to live in peace with everyone, as
much as possible.

If someone is acting silly, or they just "bug" you, hold your
tongue and keep the peace. "Depart from evil and do good;
seek peace and pursue it" (Psalm 34:14 NKJV). The "evil" you
need to depart from is nagging, picking fights, and gossiping.
The "good" is holding your tongue, or speaking words of
encouragement. You are to seek peace and *pursue* it. It won't
just fall in your lap. You have to diligently go after peace.

You are to live peacefully with people *if* it is possible, but it's not always possible. First, some
people simply like to fight and make trouble.
Sometimes they're bored, and they find it
entertaining to stir up turmoil. Avoid
them. Second, it's not always possible to
do the right thing and still get along with
everyone. If a person is doing something
clearly wrong (like lying or cheating), then

speak up. You are to keep the peace, but not at any price.

If Amber is shopping with Caitlin, and Amber thinks the new shoes Caitlin bought are ugly, she needs to live in peace by keeping her opinion to herself. But it's a different matter if she sees Caitlin steal from the shoe store. Yes, it will make Caitlin upset and angry if Amber confronts her, but it would be wrong for Amber to go along with it and keep quiet. Sometimes we keep silent (or keep the peace) about a wrong behavior so that we won't lose a friendship or lose acceptance. This is a wrong reason to live in peace.

Peace is a fruit of the Holy Spirit, and it takes time and patience to grow fruit. Do your part to live in peace with all people.

Did You Know ...

the wisdom that comes from God is peace-loving? It is also considerate and sincere. Read more in James 3:16–18.

God Talk:

"Lord, I know I don't always promote peace around me. Please help me to be patient and peace-loving with those I'm with. Please help me to know when— and when *not*—to speak up. Thank you. Amen."

More To Explore:

Proverbs 12:20 and Colossians 3:14–15

Girl Talk:

Do you like to have peace in your life? Do you think life is boring if things aren't stirred up? Who is someone you need to make peace with?

Devotion #45

"You should behave instead like God's very own children, adopted into his family—calling him 'Father, dear Father.'"
—Romans 8:15 (NLT)

Who Am I?

If you've accepted Jesus as your Savior, then you've been adopted into God's family. You've been taken in as a member, with all the rights of any other son or daughter. And you have the privilege and honor to call God your Father.

Nicole sometimes felt like a big nobody. At school, she was laughed at. At home, unless she forgot to do her chores, her parents seemed to forget she existed. But Nicole knew Jesus. He'd been her Savior since she was eight years old. Because of that, Nicole was somebody special.

If you you don't feel special or loved or important, remember who you are in Christ:

- I am Christ's friend. (John 15:15)

- Jesus chose me to bear good fruit for him. (John 15:16)

- I am a temple, or home, for God. His Spirit lives in me. (1 Corinthians 3:16; 6:19)
- I am God's workmanship (or handiwork), created in Christ to do his work that he planned beforehand that I should do. (Ephesians 2:10)
- I am chosen of God and dearly loved. (Colossians 3:12)
- I am now a child of God. I will resemble Christ when he returns. (1 John 3:1–2)

Memorize one or more of these verses. Then, when you're in a situation that makes you feel like a nobody, speak those verses right out loud. You're a daughter of the King. You've been adopted into his royal family. You're *very* special to God.

Did You Know ...

that Jesus was basically adopted by Joseph? God is Jesus' Father, but from the day he was born, Mary and Joseph were his human parents. Until Jesus was thirty, everyone thought he was Joseph's son. Read about what Jesus' earthly parents did for him in Luke 2.

More To Explore: Ephesians 1:4–5

Girl Talk:

Do you ever feel ignored or unloved? What do you do when you feel unimportant? What verse will you memorize now for help later?

God Talk:

"Lord, sometimes I feel like no one loves me. Please help me remember that you always love me, that I am important to you. Thank you for loving me. Amen."

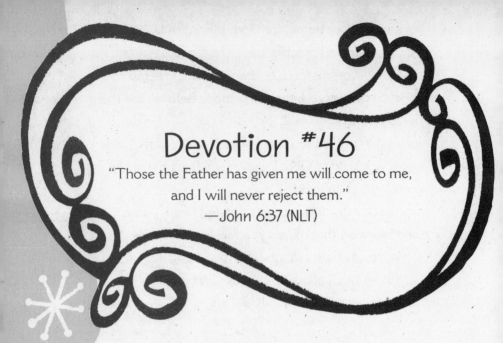

Devotion #46

"Those the Father has given me will come to me,
and I will never reject them."
—John 6:37 (NLT)

Acceptance Guaranteed

Jesus said he would never reject or push away anyone who trusted in him. We just need to go to him. He knows we aren't perfect, but he approves of us and accepts us and lives in us! No matter who on this earth rejects you, Jesus will never reject you.

We all want the acceptance and approval of friends and family members. Rejection is one of the hardest, most painful things we have to endure in this life. Classmates may reject us because we look different, or have little money.

Family members may treat us with scorn or disregard our wishes and opinions, almost as if we're invisible.

The worst rejection, however, is when we reject ourselves. We decide that because someone else doesn't like us or accept us that there must be something wrong with us. Many of us are very gifted and talented—in art, music, writing, singing. But we're afraid to express ourselves because we fear the rejection of others. What will they think of us? Will they laugh and point fingers?

Jesus accepts you just the way you are. He knew you weren't perfect when he saved you. He knows you have weaknesses and that you make mistakes. Even so, he will never reject you. Nothing can ever come between you and God's love for you. "I am convinced that nothing can ever separate us from his love. Death can't, and life can't. The angels can't, and the demons can't. Our fears for today, our worries about tomorrow, and even the powers of hell can't keep God's love away" (Romans 8:38 NLT).

Spend time with the Lord. His love will transform your life.

Did You Know ...

that even a thief who believed in Jesus in the last moments of his life went to heaven? Jesus accepted him just as he was. Read Luke 23:40–43.

More To Explore: Matthew 11:28 and John 17:12

Girl Talk:

Have you ever felt rejected by someone? Did you feel there was something wrong with you to be rejected? Did you ask God to help you with those feelings?

God Talk:

"Lord, when I'm rejected by someone, I feel so unworthy. I know you love me no matter what. Please help me remember that you care for me and that I'm worth a lot to you! Thank you! Amen."

Devotion #47

"If you remain in me and my words remain in you,
ask whatever you wish, and it will be given you."
—John 15:7 (NIV)

Heavenly Santa Claus?

Jesus himself said that if we stay joined to him, and his words continue to live in us, that we can make any request we desire, and it will be granted to us! That is one awesome promise!

Lily wanted so much to have a new jacket like her friends had—neon colored with a hood. She knew that God had promised to meet all her needs, so she prayed and prayed for that new jacket. She never did get it though. And we don't always get what we pray for. Why?

It might be that you've asked for something that's not God's will for your life. People tend to concentrate on the "asking and receiving" part. But the Bible says IF you remain and abide in Jesus—and if his words remain and stay in you—THEN you can ask what you desire and be assured of the answer. When we abide or live in him (and not just visit occasionally), we are trusting him all the time, learning from him, leaning on him, reading and studying his Word daily, and in frequent prayer about things. We are searching to know the mind of Christ.

As we do this day by day, our will (our desires) is joined with his. His desires become our desires; our concerns become the same as his. More of our prayers are according to God's will, so more are answered. Very often he changes our desires to match his. We become like Jesus as we abide in him. The more we get to know him, the more fruit he produces in our lives.

Can anyone really ever have such a close relationship with Jesus? The Bible says we can—IF we are willing to take the time to get to know him. Why not try it?

Did You Know ...

that people often delight themselves in what they want instead of the Lord? The opposite is supposed to be true. Psalm 37:4 (NIV) says, "Delight yourself in the LORD and he will give you the desires of your heart."

More To Explore: Deuteronomy 6:6–9 and Proverbs 4:4

Girl Talk:

When you pray, do you stick to the "asking for what you want" part? Do you ever ask God what he wants for you?

God Talk:

"Lord, I know I ask for many things, but I don't listen to you like I should. Please help me to listen and follow you first. I know you will give me what I really need. Thank you. Amen."

Devotion #48

"One day Jesus was praying in a certain place.
When he finished, one of his disciples said to him,
'Lord, teach us to pray.'"
—Luke 11:1 (NIV)

Learning To Pray

Jesus had the habit of prayer, of talking to his
Father, praising him and asking him for things. After
one of these prayer times, a disciple asked Jesus to teach
them how to pray too.

Morgan's Sunday school teacher challenged the whole
class to pray at least ten minutes every day that week. But
each time Morgan sat down with her timer to pray, her mind
went blank. She felt guilty, but she couldn't think of anything
to say. Her mom gave her a seven-minute formula for
prayer, but Morgan felt silly using it. She didn't have any
success with prayer as long as she tried to copy
someone else's prayer method.

Don't try to imitate someone else's prayer
life. We're all different, and our prayer lives
will be different. Our life circumstances
are different too. Your grandmother who
lives alone might pray two hours every
morning. You'd have to get up at 4:00 a.m.
to do that and still get to school on time.

Don't compare your prayer times to anyone else's. Instead, talk to God. Ask him to teach you how to pray, how much to pray, what to pray for, and how to listen for his answers.

Don't be shy about asking God for help with your prayer life. He's willing to help you with anything. "Let us come boldly to the throne of our gracious God. There we will receive his mercy, and we will find grace to help us when we need it" (Hebrews 4:16 NLT).

If you need help with your prayer life, be honest with God. Begin by saying, "Lord, teach me to pray."

Did You Know ...

that there are several examples of Jesus' escaping the crowds and going off to pray? If it was important for Jesus, it is most important for you! Read Luke 6:12; 9:18; and 9:28.

Girl Talk:

How often do you pray? Do you know what to say, or do you find yourself stumbling along? Have you asked God for help?

God Talk:

"Lord, I feel so lucky to be able to talk to you whenever I need to. I'm not always sure what to say. Please help me find the words. I want a better prayer life with you. Thank you for always being there. Amen."

More To Explore: Psalm 19:14 and Romans 8:26

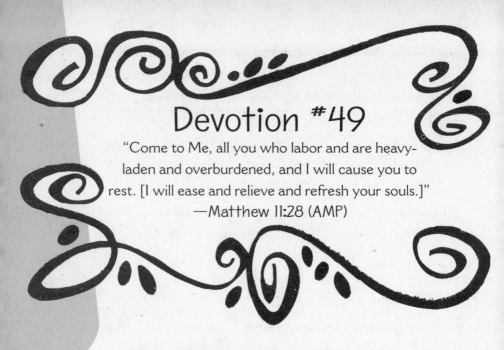

Devotion #49

"Come to Me, all you who labor and are heavy-
laden and overburdened, and I will cause you to
rest. [I will ease and relieve and refresh your souls.]"
—Matthew 11:28 (AMP)

Rested and Refreshed

Are you tired to the bone? Do you feel weighed down
by too much work or responsibility? Then Jesus says to
come to him. He will put you in a resting position! He will
support and steady you so you can take a breather. He will
make things easier and free you from your duties for a while
and refresh your mind and your emotions.

Annette came home from school with a headache, afraid
that she hadn't done well on her social studies test. Her
legs hurt from running a mile in gym class. She fixed
her little brother a snack and was ready to collapse
when the phone rang. "I'll be late tonight,
honey," her mom said. "Can you fix
spaghetti and have it ready by six?"
Annette hung up and leaned against the
table. She felt overburdened.
Some days we feel so overworked,
overtired, and overburdened that we
can't take it anymore. Then what should we

do? Jesus said to come to him, but how do we do that? We can come in prayer, being honest with him about how exhausted we are. That can be physical tiredness, but it can also be mental or emotional exhaustion. Our tired emotions might be overworked from dealing with fights or angry people or some upsetting event. Our minds might be exhausted from too much mental work like studying, or trying to figure out what to do about a problem. From ALL these things, Jesus wants to give you rest.

Are you overtired? Then take five or ten minutes, close your eyes, and breathe deeply. Ask Jesus to refresh your mind, body, and emotions. Soak it up. Take your time. Ahhhh . . .

Did You Know . . .

that you will find rest for your soul by finding the right path? Jeremiah 6:16 says that you need to find the straight and narrow road God wants you to follow. If you stay on it, rest will come.

Girl Talk:

Have you felt really tired this past week? Why do you think you were so worn down? Did you know you can rest in Jesus?

More To Explore: Isaiah 61:3 and Matthew 11:29–30

God Talk:

"Lord, I'm so tired. My body and mind need to be refreshed. Please give me rest. Please help me stay rested by staying close to you. Thank you. Amen."

Devotion #50

"Jesus said to the people who believed in him, 'You are truly my disciples if you keep obeying my teachings. And you will know the truth, and the truth will set you free.'"

—John 8:31-32 (NLT)

Three Easy Steps Toward a Better You

Do you feel trapped? Do you need freedom from something? If you're a believer, obey Jesus' teachings. Then you will learn the truth deep down where it counts—and it's this truth that will set you free from bondage.

Dawn made friends easily, but she lost them fast. Dawn had a "short fuse" and exploded in anger over minor things. She didn't give her friends a chance to explain why they were late or what they meant by something they said. Dawn was tired of losing friends, but she felt trapped by her short temper.

You can be trapped or a slave to depression, fear, a bad temper, an overspending habit, and gossip. The answer is the same, no matter what you need freedom from: learn the truth, obey, and be set free. The behavior comes *before* the feeling of freedom.

Do you have a short temper that ruins relationships? Be set free!

1. Get the truth from God's Word: "Dear friends, be quick to listen, slow to speak, and slow to get angry" (James 1:19 NLT).

2. Believe the truth: No matter how strong your feelings are, believe the truth. Your feelings may scream, "He makes me so mad! I can't stop the words from coming out!" Your feelings are not the truth. God's Word is the truth. And it says that you CAN be quick to listen, slow to speak, and slow to get angry.

3. Take action: Change the behavior. First, pray for help. Then work on specific actions. (Count to ten before speaking, or leave the room. Ask questions to get all the facts.)

Feel the freedom! Strong feelings can be slow to change. But whatever you need freedom from, the steps are the same. Today, search God's Word and find the truth that will set you free.

Did You Know ...

that you can be a slave to righteousness instead? Let God be your loving Master! Read Romans 6:14–18.

More To Explore: Romans 8:2

Girl Talk:

Do you feel trapped by something? What have you tried to do about it?

God Talk:

"Lord, I feel trapped by _____. Please help me be free from this. I need your help. With you by my side, I will conquer this! Thank you. Amen."

Devotion #51

"David talked to some others standing there to verify the report. 'What will a man get for killing this Philistine and putting an end to his abuse of Israel?' he asked them. 'Who is this pagan Philistine anyway, that he is allowed to defy the armies of the living God?' And David received the same reply as before: 'What you have been hearing is true. That is the reward for killing the giant.'"
—1 Samuel 17:26–27 (NLT)

Reaching Goals: Get a Clear Picture

A giant, Goliath, was making fun of the Israelite army. David, a shepherd boy, heard that the king had offered a reward for killing the giant (including marriage to one of the king's daughters). David checked with the soldiers to see if that was true. He also asked them why the giant was allowed to challenge and resist the Israelite army, the army of the living God.

David's goal was to do what none of the soldiers had been able to do: face the giant, Goliath, and kill him for the king. But David didn't immediately run to attack Goliath. He talked to the soldiers, he learned what Goliath had been doing to them for forty days, and he learned what reward had been offered. He took time to get a clear picture of the situation.

Do you get an idea for something you'd like to do, and then rush into it without thinking or talking to others (especially God) about it? Maybe you want to win a race at a track meet. Should you immediately start running five miles every morning before school? Or should you get a clear picture first of what's needed? What will it take to make the track team? What kind of running shoes do you need to avoid injury?

Ask questions of those in charge, and get a clear picture first. Then you'll be on your way to reaching your goal!

Did You Know ...

that Nehemiah helped rebuild the wall around Jerusalem? Nehemiah carefully judged what needed to be done, instead of rushing into the project without planning. Read Nehemiah 2:11–15.

God Talk:

"Lord, I have lots of ideas about how to live my life. Please help me to ask you first for guidance. I want to do what you want me to do. Thank you. Amen."

More To Explore: Luke 14:28

Girl Talk:

When you want to do something, do you plan it out? Or do you rush into it without thinking? Do you ask God about it? Check out *Sophie's Secret* to see what happens when Sophie and her friends go ahead with a project without approval and make a huge mess of things!

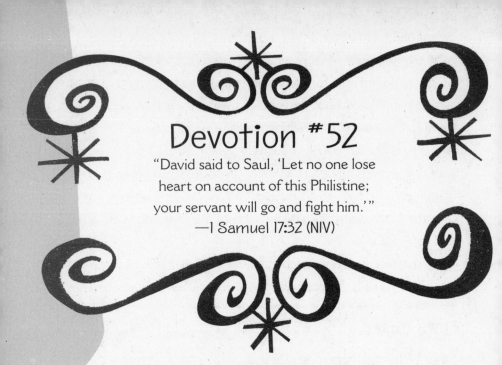

Devotion #52

"David said to Saul, 'Let no one lose
heart on account of this Philistine;
your servant will go and fight him.'"
—1 Samuel 17:32 (NIV)

Reaching Goals: Feel The Desire

You can feel David's passion and enthusiasm as he declares
to King Saul that he, David, will go and fight that insulting giant
Philistine. David encourages the soldiers not to lose heart (or
have their hearts and courage fail them). He's excited to meet
that challenge and says, "Don't worry about a thing!"

You're faced with challenges to meet too. Sara says, "I can't
wait to start the summer reading program! I plan to read
more than fifty books and win that new camera! I'm
going to the library to check out books right now.
Want to do the reading challenge with me?"

Janet says, "Sure. I guess . . . I don't have
anything better to do." Which girl has the
passionate desire to reach a goal? Who
will probably be the only one to succeed?

David's passion to fight wasn't for himself, but to strike down the giant who
mocked God and God's promises. Like David

when he faced Goliath, you also need to feel passionate about your goals. You need to feel excited about them, with enough enthusiasm to carry you through to the finish line. Half-hearted feelings and ho-hum attitudes won't be enough.

David also made a decision: "I will go and fight him." Being excited about doing something won't help unless you make a decision to accomplish it. Sara could get all excited ("I want to win that camera!"), but without a plan ("I will read fifty books. I'm going to the library now"), Sara would never meet her goal.

Don't lose heart! To reach your goals, the second thing you must do is keep your enthusiasm and excitement alive.

Did You Know ...

that only one man sounded passionate about the Israelites taking Canaan for their own? Out of twelve men sent to explore Canaan, only Caleb and Joshua felt confident. Read the story in Numbers 13:1–3, 17–20, and 26–30.

Girl Talk:

When you have something you want to do, are you excited? Do you stay excited, or do you get bored and go on to something else?

More To Explore: Deuteronomy 20:1–3 and Isaiah 35:3–4

God Talk:

"Lord, there are many things I want to do. Please help me to pray first, then plan. I want to stay excited for the plans you have for me! Thank you! Amen."

Devotion #53

"David shouted in reply, 'You come to me with sword, spear, and javelin, but I come to you in the name of the LORD Almighty—the God of the armies of Israel, whom you have defied. Today the LORD will conquer you.'" —1 Samuel 17:45–46 (NLT)

Reaching Goals: Be Confident!

When David faced Goliath, he did it with confidence. Goliath might have swords and weapons of war, but David had the living God on his side. He proclaimed without any doubt that the Lord would defeat Goliath. David was sure of God's power working through him to succeed in his goal. David spoke about the past victories God had given him. Remembering how God had delivered him from attacking lions and bears gave him confidence that God would deliver him from Goliath too.

What goals do *you* have? Do you want to learn how to in-line skate? Do you wish you could speak Spanish? Maybe you'd like to learn to dive or swim better. Whatever your goal, if you've prayed about it and are sure it's something God can approve, then be positive. Have confidence that you can achieve it.

It's not enough to say, "I hope I can." Instead, declare, "I know I can do this." Say, "I can do all things through Christ who strengthens me" (Philippians 4:13 NKJV). Repeat this when you run into difficulties as you work toward your goals. If you fall when skating, pick yourself up and quote Philippians 4:13. Do it when you belly flop your first ten dives. Say it when you have tried (and failed) to learn your Spanish ABC's.

You will also need confidence when other people question you. ("Are you SURE you want to try to dive?") Some will try to discourage you. ("You'll *never* learn to speak Spanish!") David faced this with King Saul, who doubted his ability and wanted to dress David in better armor for the fight. David's confidence helped him fight in his own way.

Don't be wishy-washy. Reach for your goals with confidence!

Did You Know . . .

that King Saul had real misgivings about sending David out to fight Goliath? David showed his confidence in God's help. Read 1 Samuel 17:33–37.

Girl Talk:

Do you have confidence that your goals are from God? If not, have you asked God for confidence in what you do?

God Talk:

"Lord, sometimes I don't feel confidence in what I do. Please help me remember that my confidence needs to be in you instead. Thank you for giving me the strength and confidence I need. Amen."

More To Explore: 2 Corinthians 3:4–5 and Psalm 27:1–3

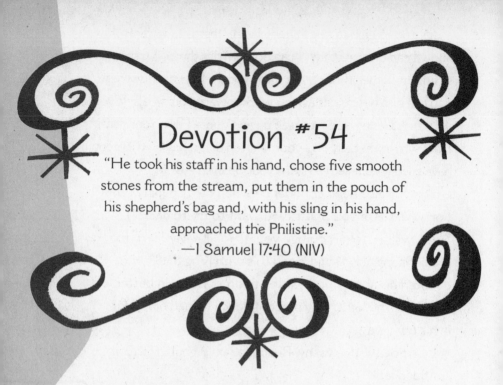

Devotion #54

"He took his staff in his hand, chose five smooth stones from the stream, put them in the pouch of his shepherd's bag and, with his sling in his hand, approached the Philistine."
—1 Samuel 17:40 (NIV)

Reaching Goals: Take Action!

David didn't have any fancy, high-tech weapons, but he had a plan. He took his shepherd's staff (a long, thick stick) and went to the stream. There, he found five smooth stones, which he placed in his large shepherd's bag. With his sling (a weapon used to hurl the stones), David walked up to the giant, Goliath.

To meet your goals, you will also need to take some action steps. If you want to learn to swim, those steps might include buying a bathing suit, signing up for classes at the Y, and reading a book on swimming techniques. If you want to learn to paint with watercolors, it might include these action steps: study how-to books by painters, buy paints and an easel, take a beginner's painting class at school, or visit an artist's studio.

It's great to have a clear idea of what your goal is, lots of desire to accomplish it, and tons of confidence. But unless you take come clear steps of action, your goal will never come to pass. David wasn't just confident. He (1) grabbed his staff, (2) went to the stream, (3) found five smooth stones to put in his bag, (4) grasped his sling, and (5) ran up to Goliath. If you want to reach goals—whatever they might be—you'll need to take action steps too. Enthusiasm won't take you very far. It's like a car without gas—nice, but not going anywhere.

Map out a clear plan of action, then take your first step!

Did You Know ...

that a famous queen saved the Jews from destruction with a very careful, thought-out plan of action? Read about Queen Esther's plan in Esther 4–7.

More To Explore: Judges 20:16

Girl Talk:

Think of something you want to do. Have you made any plans on how to make it happen? Have you set deadlines for your goal?

God Talk:

"Lord, I really want these goals to happen. Help me to make a plan to get them done. Thank you for your support that never ends. Amen."

Fun Factoid:

A sling-stone, like the ones David used, were usually somewhat larger than a baseball. They could weigh a pound or more and be thrown at 90 to 100 miles an hour!

Devotion #55

"As the Philistine moved closer to attack him,
David ran quickly toward the battle
line to meet him." —1 Samuel 17:48 (NIV)

Reaching Goals: Make a Deadline

The giant, Goliath, boldly moved closer to David to
attack and kill him. David didn't run away, or call for help,
or change his mind about his "sling and stone" plan. Instead,
he knew that the time had come to take action. So he ran
quickly to meet the Philistine, Goliath, at the battle line.

David didn't just have confidence and an action plan. He "ran
quickly toward the battle line" when Goliath moved closer. He
didn't say, "Well, some day soon I should do something about
that giant." No, he gave himself a deadline. Goliath had
already been mocking and jeering the Israelite army for
forty days. David decided it was time to act *now*—
not someday when he felt more like it.

You need deadlines too. If your goal is to
learn watercolor painting, put deadlines
for your action steps on the calendar.
Sign up for those art classes; put the date
of the first class on your calendar. Call
that local artist, set up a time to visit his
studio, and put that date on your calendar.

Decide that you're going to have all your supplies gathered by the end of the month, and write that on your calendar.

If you're vague about when you want to meet your goals, they won't happen. Saying that "some day" you're going to volunteer to help in the church nursery, or "any day now" you plan to learn to play guitar isn't enough. Instead, write down the date you expect to achieve your goal. And put down time limits for each individual step too. (It's fine if it takes you longer than you think it will.) Having a deadline will motivate you to get started *now*.

Do you have a goal that excites you? Then write down a deadline for meeting it on your calendar. You're well on your way now!

Did You Know ...

that giving yourself a "false deadline" may help you meet the deadline? You write the false deadline down four days before the actual deadline, so you won't have a last-minute rush to complete a project.

Girl Talk:

Do you have projects started but not finished? Would a deadline help?

More To Explore: Psalm 112:7 and Isaiah 26:3-4

God Talk:

"Lord, I have good intentions, but I don't always finish what I start. Help me stay focused and finish my projects.

Thank you for your loving care.

Amen."

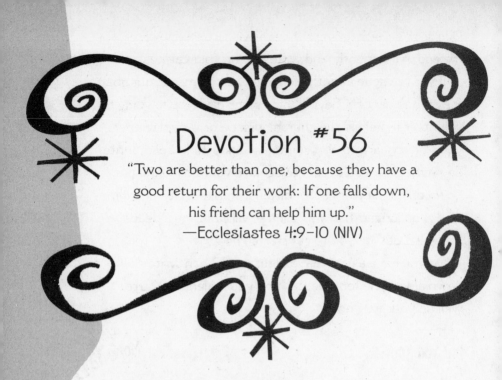

Devotion #56

"Two are better than one, because they have a
good return for their work: If one falls down,
his friend can help him up."
—Ecclesiastes 4:9-10 (NIV)

Reaching Goals: Get Support

Some goals, especially small ones that can be done today
or very soon, you can do alone. But large goals are easier to
reach if you get help and support from others. Two working
together are better than each person working alone. When
someone helps or assists you, their efforts will be joined with
yours for an even better yield or outcome.

Suppose your goal is to train your singing voice so you
can sing solos at church or school some day. You can
work alone, but how much better to ask for the
support and help of your family, your music
teacher at school, or your youth leader.
Support from your parents might include
private voice lessons. Your music
teacher might give you extra practice
time after school. Your youth leader
might find opportunities for you to sing
(when you're ready).

Way back in Genesis 2:18, God said it wasn't good for a man (or a girl) to be alone. He knows we do better with help, so don't be ashamed or shy about asking for support. Even Jesus sent his disciples out two by two when it was time for them to minister (Mark 6:7). You'll be able to reach your goals much easier (and have encouragement on the days you want to quit) if you enlist help from other people.

Your ultimate help and support, of course, comes from God. He's available 24/7, while people aren't. If this is a God-given, God-approved goal, he also has the power to see that you're in the right place at the right time.

Look for help in reaching your goals, and be sure to help *others* reach theirs!

Did You Know ...

that the church body works better when people work together rather than alone? Everyone is important, and everyone needs the support of the others. Read 1 Corinthians 12:12–13, 18–21.

Girl Talk:

Is there something you are working toward right now? Who do you think can help you achieve your goal? Someone at home, school, or church?

More To Explore: Exodus 4:10–16 and Numbers 11:10–17

God Talk:

"Lord, I thank you for giving me such big dreams. Please help me find the right people to help me. Thank you for your love and support. Amen."

Devotion #57

"Let us not become weary in doing good, for at the proper time we will reap a harvest if we do not give up."
—Galatians 6:9 (NIV)

Reaching Goals: Be Persistent

When we start something new, we feel energetic. But on the way to meeting our goal, we will need to be persistent (never stopping, performing the same day by day). Don't get tired of doing the necessary things to meet your goal, even if it takes more time than you planned. At the right and proper time, you *will* meet that goal, but only if you don't give up.

If your goal is to join the sixth-grade track team, you may start out with great enthusiasm. You lift weights three times a week, you jog in the morning before school, and you eat protein snacks. Several weeks into your program, though, you may find yourself bored, or tired of the routine, or just sick of eating chicken when you'd rather have French fries. If you give up at this point, you won't reach your goal. However, if you pray for help and focus again on your end result, you will get past this temptation to quit.

When you're on your way to meeting your goals, be careful not to get distracted by things that catch your attention, but aren't really that important. Being distracted can make you give up on your goal almost without realizing it. It's so easy to do! Remember when Jesus visited the home of Mary and Martha? Imagine having the Lord come to your home to talk! "But Martha was distracted by all the preparations that had to be made" (Luke 10:40 NIV). She was paying so much attention to the housework and cooking that she didn't focus on the important thing: Jesus had come to see her! So focus on the main goal.

And when you're tempted to quit, don't! Keep on keepin' on!

Did You Know ...

that Jesus told a great parable about an unjust judge? This judge didn't want to take up his time dealing with a woman's complaint. See what Jesus says about it in Luke 18:1–8.

Girl Talk:

When there is something you really want, do you stick to it through thick and thin? Or do all kinds of things sidetrack you?

More To Explore: 1 Corinthians 15:58 and James 5:7–8

God Talk:

"Lord, this dream I have is a lot of work. Help me to stay focused: on you, and on what I want to do. Please help me stay free of distractions. Thank you! Amen."

Devotion #58

"You are still [unspiritual, having the nature] of the flesh [under the control of ordinary impulses]. For as long as [there are] envying and jealousy and wrangling and factions among you, are you not unspiritual and of the flesh, behaving yourselves after a human standard and like mere (unchanged) men?"
—1 Corinthians 3:3 (AMP)

Reaching Goals: Manage Your Emotions

When you give in and are guided by your emotions, or those "ordinary impulses," all kinds of trouble results. People become jealous, they argue loud and long, and they take sides against one another. If you are a follower of Christ, this should not be your behavior.

When you first announce to your friends or family that you're attempting a certain goal, you may get very unspiritual reactions. Some may express mild doubt that eats at your self-confidence. ("Are you *sure* you want to try learning Spanish?") Others will be openly negative. ("I don't think you have a chance of making the team.") Still others—jealous of your dream—can be downright nasty. ("Are you crazy? You're nuts to think you can ever sing in public.") Discouraging put-downs like this can make you want to quit.

It's sad, but true, that not all people will applaud your goals and dreams. People with low self-esteem—people who don't feel good about themselves—try to make themselves feel better by pulling you down. Don't listen to their discouraging comments! Remember: "I can do all things through Christ who strengthens me" (Philippians 4:13 NKJV). Control your emotional reactions to these negative comments. Pray and don't say anything until you're calm. Don't defend yourself. Simply say, "I'm sorry you feel that way," and change the subject.

Then be doubly determined to lean on God to see you through to victory!

Did You Know ...

that you need to watch out for your own reactions? You should not be jealous of someone else's goal and success. Read Acts 13:45 to see what happened when Paul was speaking.

Girl Talk:

Who do you usually go to for advice and help? Do these people come through for you, or do their remarks drag you down? Who can you turn to and count on for support?

More To Explore: James 3:16 and I Corinthians 12:25-26

God Talk:

"Lord, you know I have dreams. Not everyone thinks I can make it. Please help me to stay focused on you and what you want me to do. Thank you for being with me through the good and the bad. Amen."

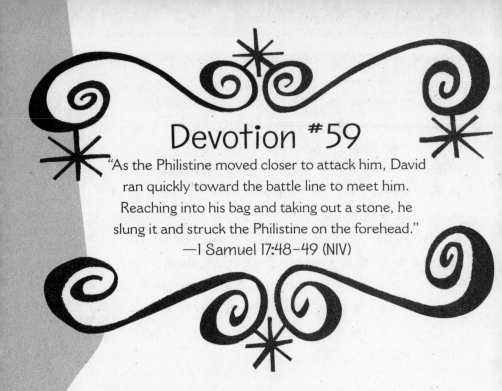

Devotion #59

"As the Philistine moved closer to attack him, David
ran quickly toward the battle line to meet him.
Reaching into his bag and taking out a stone, he
slung it and struck the Philistine on the forehead."
—1 Samuel 17:48–49 (NIV)

Reaching Goals: Take Courage

After talking and planning and preparing, David went up
against the giant, Goliath, all alone. The giant was covered in
his armor, while David had a rock for a weapon. He took
courage, slung a rock at the giant, and met his goal. Goliath
fell down dead, and Israel's army was saved.

When you are trying to achieve your goals, it's good to
have the support and encouragement of others. But at
some point, after all the planning and practicing,
you have to take action all alone. You stand at
the microphone and sing that solo—alone. You
run that race—alone. You paint that
picture, or write that story, or ride that
horse, or get on that bike—alone. This
takes courage. Without it, you won't
meet your goal, even if you've faithfully
followed every step until now.

Fear is a normal feeling at this point, but it's what you do with this feeling that counts. You can do like King Saul and his army when they were faced with Goliath's threats. "When Saul and the Israelites heard this, they were terrified and deeply shaken" (1 Samuel 17:11 NLT). For forty days, Saul and his men let their fear of being defeated keep them from facing Goliath. No doubt David, as a young shepherd boy, had fearful feelings as he faced the giant. But David didn't focus on his fear and let it paralyze him. Instead, he took courage from the living God and "ran quickly toward the battle line" to meet Goliath.

When you need courage to take action, pray first. Then move ahead and reach that goal!

Did You Know ...

that an angel said, "Fear not!" to many people God gave a job to do? God wanted them to know they didn't need to be afraid, that God was with them in their task. Read Luke 1:13, 30; and 2:10.

More To Explore: Psalm 27:1 and Proverbs 28:1

Girl Talk:

Are you getting close to reaching a goal or dream? How much of a hold does fear have on you? Do you feel ready to finish?

God Talk:

"Lord, thank you for all your love and support as I have worked toward _____. Please give me the courage to finish it! I love you. Amen."

Devotion #60

"The battle is the LORD's."
—1 Samuel 17:47 (NIV)

Reaching Goals: Lean on God

Just before the battle with Goliath in 1 Samuel 17, David announced to one and all that he expected God to win this battle for him. "The LORD will . . . deliver me" (v. 37), "This day the LORD will hand you [Goliath] over to me" (v. 46), and "The LORD saves" (v. 47). David was well aware that in his own strength, he was no match at all for Goliath. Yes, David had to step up to the battle line himself. He also totally depended on God to save him, "for the battle is the LORD's."

Because of different personalities, most believers go to extremes. Sarah sits back, does nothing but pray, and says she's "just trusting the Lord" to give her good grades. (No, she's not. She's being lazy.) Wendy works hard from dawn to dusk, rarely prays, and believes she will succeed someday in the music field based on her own talent. (No, she won't. She's arrogant and thinks she doesn't need God's help for anything.) Be careful that you don't fall into error either way.

Successfully reaching your goals depends on two things that might, at first, seem like opposites. You need to do the work necessary to reach your goals, praying each step of the way. But you also need to understand that it is God who will give you the power to succeed. You must be prepared, but it is God who saves and provides. "The horse is prepared for the day of battle, but deliverance is of the LORD" (Proverbs 21:31 NKJV). To reach your goals, find the balance. You can't sit idle, expecting God to do the work for you. But you won't succeed in God's plans for your life if you trust in yourself, thinking you're so clever or so smart you don't need God's help.

Do plan, be persistent, and be confident. Then, leaning on God, take action—for the battle is the Lord's.

Did You Know . . .

that God told King Jehoshaphat to be ready for a battle, but he wouldn't have to fight it? See what the king decided to do in 2 Chronicles 20:15–21.

Girl Talk:

How often do you pray for God's guidance? Do you sit back and wait, or do you work and prepare?

More To Explore: Psalm 44:6–7 and Zechariah 4:6

God Talk:

"Lord, I believe my goal of _____ is from you. Help me to be prepared to finish it. Thank you for your support that never ends. Amen."

Devotion #61

"Being confident of this very thing, that He who has begun a good work in you will complete it until the day of Jesus Christ." —Philippians 1:6 (NKJV)

Confidence in ME?

Be very sure—be confident—that God lives in you. He is working in you to mature you, and he will keep working until you're finally finished—complete and perfect.

Heather was a believer, but she didn't feel confident. She tried to ignore the girls in band who laughed when her clarinet squeaked. She pretended not to mind when the gym teacher yelled, "Come on, Slowpoke!" as they ran around the track. She turned her back on her brother after school when he called her "Tubby." But when Heather fell into bed that night, it all came rushing back. She felt untalented, fat, and slow.

She was, in fact, NONE of those things. But the opinions of others can sometimes beat down our self-confidence.

You are a child of God. He lives in you and is working in you. You can be confident of that! To feel better about yourself, be sure to do the following things:

- Never speak negatively about yourself.
- Think about and speak positive things about yourself.
- Never compare yourself with others.
- Find something you like to do—something you're good at—and practice it over and over.
- You and God together determine your worth; don't let someone else do it.
- Stay close to God, your true source of confidence.

God is living and working in you every minute of your life. You can be confident of that!

Did You Know ...

that the author of Hebrews writes a wonderful blessing at the end of his letter? "May the God of peace . . . equip you with everything good for doing his will." Read the entire blessing in Hebrews 13:20–21 (NIV).

Girl Talk:

Do you ever feel like your confidence is missing? Do you realize how much God loves you? What is one thing you can do to feel more confident today?

More To Explore: Philippians 2:13

God Talk:

"Lord, when things don't go right, I can feel down really easily. Please help me to remember that all I need is you. Thank you for your confidence in me that never ends. I love you! Amen."

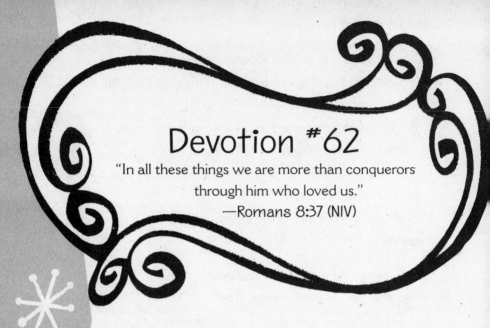

Devotion #62

"In all these things we are more than conquerors
through him who loved us."
—Romans 8:37 (NIV)

On To Victory!

No matter what kind of trouble or challenge you face
right now, overwhelming victory is yours through Christ.
Not just enough victory to survive or get by. No! A *super-*
strong victory, through Jesus, who loves and lives in you.

The key to having victory in our lives—instead of becoming victims of others or bad circumstances—is Jesus. It is only
through him that success is ours. As you lean on him and
trust him to give you whatever you need, you will learn by
experience that you CAN do all things through Christ,
who gives you the strength (Philippians 4:13).

What kind of hard situation are you facing? Has
someone in your family discovered they have
a serious disease? Has your dad changed
jobs, forcing you to move across the
country? Did you gain a lot of weight
over the summer and don't want to face
the teasing of your classmates? Do you
have an older brother or sister in trouble
with the law? Do you live in a dangerous

neighborhood? No matter what you face, you are *still* more than a conqueror.

God is all-powerful—more than enough for any trouble or circumstance—and his Spirit lives in us. "I will ask the Father, and He will give you another Helper, that He may be with you forever" (John 14:16 NASB). The Holy Spirit in us is our helper. As you spend time with God and talk to him and share your fears, you'll draw strength from him. Instead of focusing on the problem, keep your attention on Jesus, the problem solver.

Then be ready for a sweeping victory!

Did You Know ...

that even in prison, Joseph was victorious? God blessed every-thing Joseph did, and the prison warden put him in charge of everyone in the prison! Read Genesis 39.

Girl Talk:

Are you going through a tough situation right now? In the past? Did you handle it alone? How could you handle it better with God's help?

More To Explore: Deuteronomy 20:4 and John 16:33

God Talk:

"Lord, I'm really worried about _____. I don't know what to do, but I know you will get me through this. Please help me to stay calm and trust in you. Thank you for always being there for me. Amen."

Devotion #63

"Cultivate inner beauty, the gentle,
gracious kind that God delights in."
—1 Peter 3:4 (MSG)

God Knows You Inside Out

Nurture the growth of inner qualities of kindness and tenderness. Be soft and mild, with a generous spirit, not harsh or stern or severe. This is what God delights in.

Brittany dressed in the latest fashions, had her hair fixed like her favorite movie star's, and had a sharp, clever remark for everyone. It really irritated her that her neighbor, Beth (who was plain and ordinary-looking), had more friends. Brittany's own sister had the nerve to say she wished Brittany was more like Beth! But why? Brittany had no idea.

It's all about beauty. We have an outer life that everyone can see. What others think of us is determined by our outer life. But we have an inner life too, which God sees. Our reputation with God is based on our heart, or inner life. We tend to give 90 percent of our attention to our outer life, and very little to our inner life. But God doesn't watch just our actions. He examines the attitudes, motives, and desires of our heart. All these things are important to him—and to others.

The inner person is who we *really* are. People will call you a phony when your outer behavior (acting sweetsy-sweet) doesn't match your attitude (resentful or superior). And you will feel like a fake when you do one thing while feeling something different. True inner beauty will also be seen and appreciated on the outside.

Did You Know ...

that Jesus once compared the hypocritical Pharisees to dead bones in beautiful tombs? Jesus said they were pretty on the outside, but full of dead bones on the inside. Read Matthew 23:27.

More To Explore: I Samuel 16:7 and Luke 16:15

Girl Talk:

Does the way you act match how you feel on the inside? Would you be embarrassed if others could see the real you?

God Talk:

"Lord, my heart doesn't always match what I say and do. Thank you for helping me get rid of the bad attitudes in my heart. Amen."

Mini-Quiz

What would a girl with inner beauty do when her friend gives her an ugly choker?

(a) Say, "Even my mom wouldn't wear that!"

(b) Say, "Thank you! I'll wear this with my new shirt!"

(c) Exchange the choker for a necklace she liked.

(Did you pick *b*? If not, then read this devotion again!)

Devotion #64

"Trust in the LORD with all your heart;
do not depend on your own understanding."
—Proverbs 3:5 (NLT)

Battling Bewilderment

Life can be confusing. Sometimes we just don't
know what to do. Learn to lean on, trust in, and be confident in the Lord. Trust him with your whole heart and
mind. Don't depend on figuring things out yourself.

Do you ever wonder what God is doing in your life? You've
prayed about the things that worry you, or the situations
causing you distress, but nothing seems to be happening. You
still can't get along with your stepsister. Your grades in math
are slipping, no matter how hard you pray and study. Do
you ever try hard to figure things out instead of praying? (*What if I do this? No, I'll do that first, then I'll
do this. But then, if I do that, what will happen
over here?*) That kind of thinking—depending on your own mind—will only make
you confused, anxious, and afraid.

As believers, we have the privilege of
staying peaceful in the middle of trying
times. We can trust in God even when we
don't understand what has already happened,

or what is going to happen in the future. We can "rest in the LORD, and wait patiently for Him" (Psalm 37:7 NKJV).

Sometimes tragedies strike. Baby brother catches a virus that attacks his lungs, and he ends up in the hospital. A tornado flattens our house. Our parents get a divorce. We are shocked and bewildered. What do we do now? Remember: *nothing* that has happened took God by surprise. He knew it was coming, he has a plan, and he'll take care of you. You don't have to figure everything out! "Trust in Him at all times, you people; pour out your heart before Him; God is a refuge for us" (Psalm 62:8 NKJV).

Learn to trust God and lean on him at all times. Trade your confusion for his peace.

Did You Know ...

that Sophie is very confused for a time about her place in her family? She's not sure who to lean on in *Sophie's Secret*.

God Talk:

"Lord, I feel really confused about _____. I don't know what to do. Please guide me and show me the way to go. Thank you for always being with me. Amen."

Girl Talk:

Do you ever feel confused when making a big decision? Do you worry over it or ask God about it?

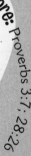

More To Explore: Proverbs 3:7; 28:26

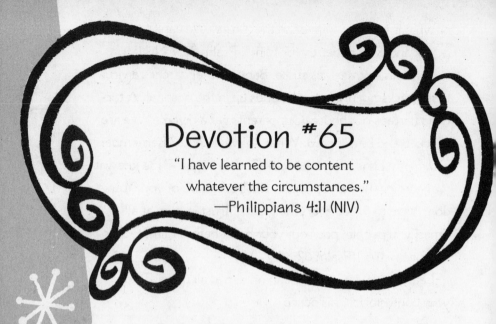

Devotion #65

"I have learned to be content
whatever the circumstances."
—Philippians 4:11 (NIV)

Crafting a Content Heart

Learn to be satisfied with how things are, no matter what is happening in your life. Whether you have too little, just enough, or more than enough, be stable and unchanging in your moods. Learn to get along happily, whether you have much or little.

Amber found it easier to be content with her life when her dad still had his high-paying job. When he was laid off, and Amber had much less, a discontented spirit set in. Over several months, though, Amber learned to be content. She learned to enjoy videos and popcorn at home with her family instead of going into the city to a show. In fact, she had to admit that she enjoyed her family a lot more every day, now that her dad was home in the evenings.

No matter what is happening, we are to tell God what we need. While waiting for the answer to arrive, focus on all the times God has helped you in the past. "Don't worry about anything; instead, pray about everything. Tell God what you need, and thank him for all he has done" (Philippians 4:6 NLT).

If you have asked God for something that is going to be good for you, he will give you what you asked for. But rest in the knowledge that if it's not right, God will do something far better than you asked for. Trust him completely to handle the situation. "Do not throw away this confident trust in the Lord, no matter what happens. Remember the great reward it brings you! Patient endurance is what you need now, so you will continue to do God's will. Then you will receive all that he has promised" (Hebrews 10:35–36 NLT).

A contented heart—free from anxious thoughts and worries—is a priceless possession. Trust God, and learn to be content.

Did You Know ...

that godliness with contentment is fantastic? First Timothy 6:6–9 says that being rich provides many temptations and pitfalls that are hard to avoid. It's easier to stay godly with less.

More To Explore: Hebrews 13:5 and Matthew 6:31–34

Girl Talk:

Do you ever feel content? Do you worry about how much you do or don't have? Have you asked God to give you contentment?

God Talk:

"Lord, I tend to think a lot about what I want but don't have. Please help me to be content with what I have. I know you will give me everything I need. Thank you. Amen."

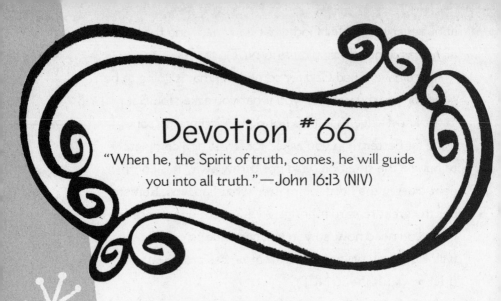

Devotion #66

"When he, the Spirit of truth, comes, he will guide you into all truth." —John 16:13 (NIV)

Saved by The Holy Spirit

One of the jobs of the Holy Spirit is to guide us. We often need help in making decisions or choosing the right path to take. The Holy Spirit (also called the Helper) wants to guide you. When you ask others for advice, they give you conflicting opinions about what to do. The Holy Spirit, however, knows the whole truth about the situation— all sides of it—and wants to help you make the *best* decision. Do you need help deciding what summer school class to take? Do you need advice for dealing with a stressed-out stepmom? Do you need help solving a money problem? The Holy Spirit will guide you.

No one learns to hear from the Holy Spirit overnight. It takes time—and learning from your mistakes. But the following things can help you "tune-up" your hearing:

- Have regular prayer time with God. Don't just talk to him. Sit and listen too.
- Be careful what you feed your mind. If you watch ungodly movies it will be

harder to tune in to the Holy Spirit's frequency.

- Be willing to do God's will, even if it's not what you want.
- Realize you will probably receive guidance one step at a time, rather than a detailed plan. As you take each obedient step, God will reveal the next step.
- Have an attitude of gratitude.
- Feed your mind on God's Word.
- Don't do anything unless you have peace in your heart about it. Pay attention to the little warning signs that the Holy Spirit sends your way. Stop and wait until you have peace.

Cooperate with the Holy Spirit, and get ready for an exciting adventure as he guides you.

Did You Know ...

that we received the Holy Spirit so we can understand what God has given us? The Holy Spirit is the teacher bringing understanding between God and us. Read 1 Corinthians 2:10–13.

Girl Talk:

Do you want help with decisions but aren't sure where to turn? Do you ask God for help but aren't sure he's answering? You can trust that he hears and cares.

More To Explore: John 14:17 and 1 John 4:6

God Talk:

"Lord, sometimes I need help, and I'm confused. I know you have the answers, if I will just listen. Please help me to be patient and wait for your answer. You are always right! Thank you. Amen."

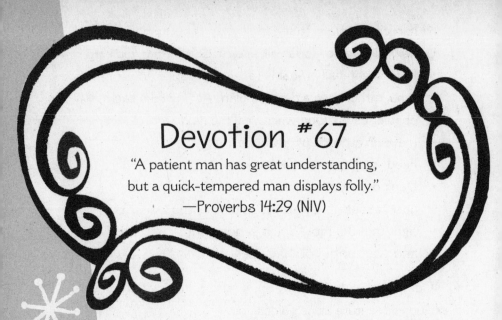

Devotion #67

"A patient man has great understanding,
but a quick-tempered man displays folly."
—Proverbs 14:29 (NIV)

I'm So Angry I Could Pray!

A person who controls her anger can make good judgments. She knows the best course of action in trying times. Someone with a quick temper will make stupid, costly, and foolish mistakes. Which girl do you want to be? Whose life will certainly be happier?

Wouldn't you like to have patience when bad things happen, or when you need help with something? Maybe you got ignored and sat on the bench the whole soccer game. Or your sister swiped the new tee you planned to wear to school today—and now it's dirty. What's the best way to handle each situation? Giving in to your anger is NOT the best way. You'll just create even bigger problems.

It's hard to know how to deal with difficult people or circumstances if you have a quick temper. It requires patience to hear from God about what to do. A quick-tempered person shoots off her mouth and takes impulsive—often destructive—actions without thinking. Much damage is done that way, and people will dislike you. "A quick-tempered man acts foolishly, and a man of wicked intentions is hated" (Proverbs 14:17 NKJV). Only if you're patient will you be able to get God's guidance about how to handle something wisely.

Feeling anger is not wrong, but expressing that anger quickly can backfire. A big step toward controlling anger is to be slow in expressing it. Stop! Be silent! Think! Pray! Tell God how angry you are—and why—and ask him for direction about what to do. Then calm down and listen. Don't do ANYTHING until you're sure what God and his Word say to do. Otherwise you may act foolishly, and some rash behavior will cause even more problems than you had before.

Endure trying circumstances with an even temper, take time to hear from God, and you'll act wisely.

Did You Know ...

that the book of Titus deals chiefly with teaching others to be self-controlled, honest, and respectful? Paul wrote this letter to Titus, who was in charge on the island of Crete. Read Titus 1:5–2:1.

More To Explore: James 1:19 and Proverbs 25:28

Girl Talk:

How often do you say something in anger without thinking? Is it hard for you to stay calm and say nothing?

God Talk:

"Lord, I know I sometimes don't control my anger very well. Please help me to stay calm and to ask you for guidance. I want to act the way you would act. Thank you. Amen."

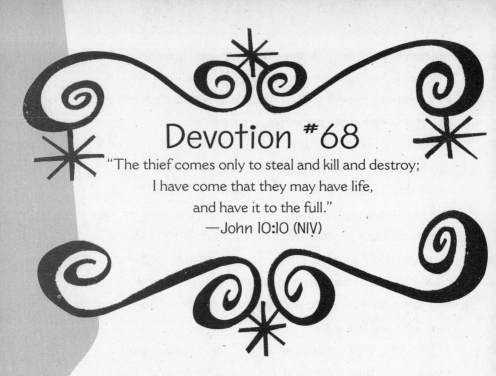

Devotion #68

"The thief comes only to steal and kill and destroy;
I have come that they may have life,
and have it to the full."
—John 10:10 (NIV)

Living The Good Life

Satan (the thief) is interested only in himself. He wants to steal (our health, our work, our peace) and to kill (our joy, our bodies) and to destroy (our families and friendships). Jesus came for the opposite reason: to give us an abundant, joy-filled life; a life overflowing with blessings.

Life has a beginning, a middle, and an ending. Your grandparents may be near the end of their lives, while you are nearer the beginning. All of life is meant to be enjoyed. Although Satan wants to ruin things for you, God wants you to enjoy the journey of your life.

Like the route for any journey or trip, life is always changing. It will be hard to enjoy your life until you understand that. Relationships are always changing—either growing or dying. Your body is growing at a rapid rate. (Just look at your baby pictures to see how you've changed!) Your schoolwork changes from year to year, getting harder. But since you've learned more, you can handle it. Sometimes God takes us through tough times because there are things we need to learn so we can more fully enjoy our lives later. No matter how good your life is right now (or how hard), it will pass. Then you'll be in a new phase to enjoy.

This time next year you'll be very different in some ways. Just don't struggle so hard trying to get to the next place that you fail to enjoy where you are right now. It's good to have goals (earning that grade, learning that ballet step, making a new friend). But remember that Jesus died so you would have a joyful, abundant life TODAY too.

Make a choice to enjoy your life to the full!

Did You Know ...

that Jesus compared himself to bread? He calls himself "the bread of life" in John 6:48–51. Does this passage remind you of Communion at church? It should!

Girl Talk:

Are you enjoying your life as it is today, or are you wishing for things that will happen in the future? What things are you enjoying *today*?

More To Explore: Luke 19:10

God Talk:

"Lord, I look forward to a lot of things in my life. Help me to enjoy today and what is happening now. Thank you for your work in my life today. Amen."

Devotion #69

"We are hard pressed on every side, but not crushed;
perplexed, but not in despair; persecuted,
but not abandoned; struck down, but not destroyed."
—2 Corinthians 4:8–9 (NIV)

A Hope-FuLL ExisTence

Life can be very hard sometimes, but if you belong to
Christ, you always have a sure hope. You may feel pres-
sured, but you won't be broken. Situations may leave you
bewildered and confused, but never without hope. You may be
suffering, but you are never deserted or left behind. You may
feel struck down temporarily, but you will never be ruined.

Some years are easy, and some years you face very fiery
trials. They might come in the form of your dad being laid
off from his job, or your sister needing heart surgery,
or your house burning down. Do you ever feel
confused by the suffering and trials you experience? It's normal to wonder why it has to
be that way and how it's all going to
work out.

Just don't be fooled into thinking you'll
be destroyed by it. You always have hope
because Jesus lives in you! This isn't the
kind of hope you find in the world, like "I hope

I get asked to that party," or "I hope it doesn't rain." That kind of hope is flimsy wishful thinking. The kind of hope *you* have is rock-solid. "May the God of hope fill you with all joy and peace as you trust in him, so that you may overflow with hope by the power of the Holy Spirit" (Romans 15:13 NIV). He's the God of hope! That's why you never have to worry, no matter what you're going through at this moment.

If you're in the middle of a heavy trial right now, talk to God frequently. Draw on his courage and hope. Then you can also say, "Yet in all these things we are more than conquerors through Him who loved us" (Romans 8:37 NKJV).

Did You Know ...

that Paul survived many, many trials, but he would boast only about his weakness? Read 2 Corinthians 11:23–30 for his amazing story.

God Talk:

"Lord, I have a rough time to get through. Help me to rely on you, knowing that I always have hope in you. Thank you for your everlasting love. Amen."

Girl Talk:

Are you going through any trials right now? Do you worry that God doesn't care, or do you talk to God about your problems?

More To Explore: 2 Corinthians 6:4–10 and Romans 5:3–5

FUN TIP:

Keep a journal. Write down your thoughts, feelings, and questions. Talk to God about them and write down his answers.

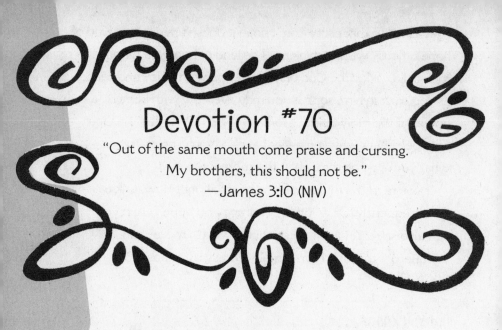

Devotion #70

"Out of the same mouth come praise and cursing.
My brothers, this should not be."
—James 3:10 (NIV)

Divided, You Will Fall

In James' letter, he described men who were praising God, yet cursing people (who are made in God's image). Thanksgiving and swearing gushed out of the same mouth. Surely, this is not good or suitable for followers of Christ!

Have you ever been guilty of sitting in church, singing praise and worship songs, then going home and using your mouth to gossip on the phone in the afternoon? Gossiping, judging, criticizing others, and faultfinding are disgusting habits to God. He doesn't want us to praise him, then turn around and pick apart the people he created.

You may have heard the term "split personality." It's a mental condition where two very different personalities appear to live inside the same person. This is what James is calling believers who say they praise God, but they also curse their fellow men. He says there's something very wrong with this picture.

This "forked tongue" tends to happen for

one of two reasons: we either think too much of ourselves (pride), or we think too little of ourselves (low self-esteem). If we're puffed up with pride, we'll look down on anyone who looks or acts differently from the way we act. (After all, if we're *right*, they must be wrong!) If we have low self-esteem, we may use our critical attitude toward others to make ourselves feel better than they are. "But," you may say, "she criticized me first!" Then what? "Bless those who persecute you; bless and do not curse" (Romans 12:14 NIV). Ouch! Hard to do, but godly, just the same.

Once we realize we're not perfect either, we'll be able to be more generous with the faults of others. Then we can heal that "split" and give praise to God and people alike.

Did You Know ...

that God told the Israelites "I have been watching!" as they acted like they had split personalities? They were committing horrible sins, but then they came into the temple and said they were safe. Read Jeremiah 7:5–11.

Girl Talk:

Do you sometimes say mean things about others, even though you know you shouldn't? Could you try to find something positive to say instead?

More To Explore: Read more in James 3:9–12.

God Talk:

"Lord, sometimes nasty things come out of my mouth. I know it's wrong. Please help me remember to say positive things or just keep my mouth quiet. Thank you for your perfect example! I love you! Amen."

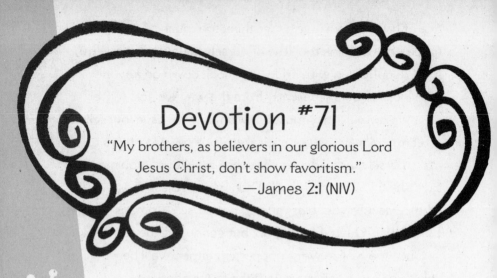

Devotion #71

"My brothers, as believers in our glorious Lord
Jesus Christ, don't show favoritism."
—James 2:1 (NIV)

Don't Play Favorites

Jesus spent time with his disciples, but he also
spent time with tax collectors, the most hated sinners
in the cities. He did not show favoritism to anyone. He
was kind and loving to all. If you say you're a follower of
Jesus, then you must act like him.

Amanda and Kylie arrived at the lunch table at the same
time. There was only one seat left. Amanda wasn't as pretty,
and her hand-me-downs (while clean) were worn. Kylie had
the latest haircut with streaks and the hottest clothes available at the mall. "This seat is saved for Kylie," several girls
said. Amanda, not surprised, went to look for another
table. She'd just been the victim of favoritism.

Favoritism—unfair treatment because of discrimination or prejudice—is hurtful. The
Bible clearly says that if you're a believer,
you shouldn't show favoritism. Treat
others the same, no matter how they
are dressed or how much money they
have. The reasons behind your actions
determine whether you are showing
favoritism or not. If you hope the wealthy

person will share his money with you (if you're nice to him), then you're only being nice to get something. That's not love—that's greed. "If you give special attention and a good seat to the rich person, but you say to the poor one, 'You can stand over there, or else sit on the floor'—well, doesn't this discrimination show that you are guided by wrong motives?" (James 2:3–4 NLT).

It hurts to be the victim of favoritism. It makes you feel as if you're not worth as much as other people. But that's never true! We all are equal in God's eyes. He never plays favorites among his children.

Be like God. Treat others with equal love and care.

Did You Know ...

that several other verses talk about judging fairly? Read Leviticus 19:15; Deuteronomy 1:17; and James 2:9.

More To Explore: James 3:17

Girl Talk:

Have you ever been rejected because of what you didn't own? Have you ever rejected someone because of what they didn't have? If so, ask for their forgiveness—and God's too!

God Talk:

"Lord, I should be content with what I have, but it's hard. Please help me to remember that you are all I really need. I want to be as kind to others as you are to me. Thank you. Amen."

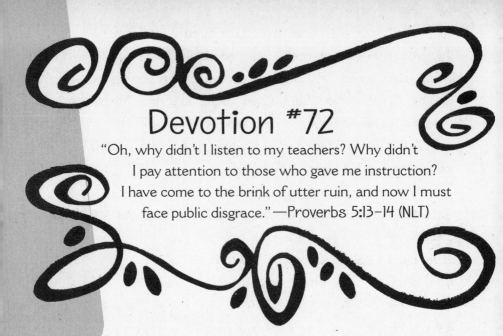

Devotion #72

"Oh, why didn't I listen to my teachers? Why didn't
I pay attention to those who gave me instruction?
I have come to the brink of utter ruin, and now I must
face public disgrace." —Proverbs 5:13–14 (NLT)

Hearing Impaired

Someone at the end of his life spoke these words.
When it was too late, he realized that the teachers in his
youth had tried to help him learn valuable lessons for life. But
he didn't pay attention and has come to ruin. Total ruin: physically, financially, and socially. His reputation is now public, and
he is disgraced and ashamed. It could have been prevented if
he'd listened as a young person to his teachers.

You have teachers at home (your parents and grandparents), at school (your instructors), and at church (Sunday school teachers, pastors, and youth leaders).

They're all trying to help you learn valuable
things so your life will be successful. Sometimes we feel these people are too old
and too "out of it" to be able to teach us
what we need to know. They didn't
grow up in our world, so how can they
know what things to teach us?
Because some things never change.

Principles for building loving relationships, gaining financial success through hard work, and taking care of our bodies don't change. Those principles are found in the Bible, and the Word of God is the same forever.

God's Word has some pretty strong words for people who won't listen to instruction and teaching. "The fear of the LORD is the beginning of knowledge, but fools despise wisdom and instruction" (Proverbs 1:7 NKJV). And "whoever loves instruction loves knowledge, but he who hates correction is stupid" (Proverbs 12:1 NKJV).

Make up your mind to love instruction. Learn the principles that will lead to a successful, happy life.

Did You Know ...

that your parents and other leaders are held accountable for you by God? God expects your parents and those in authority over you to guide you in his ways, to the best of their abilities. Read Hebrews 13:17.

More To Explore:

Proverbs 15:32 and Jeremiah 3:25

Girl Talk:

Do you listen when your parents have something to talk about with you? Do you thank your parents for guiding you?

God Talk:

"Lord, I know you gave me my mom and dad and others to help guide me in your ways. Thank you for their help in my life. Please help me to remember that they love me and want what's best for me. Thank you. Amen."

Devotion #73

"Make sure that nobody pays back wrong for wrong,
but always try to be kind to each other
and to everyone else."
—1 Thessalonians 5:15 (NIV)

Payback Time: A Tempting Trap

Christians are not to counterattack and strike back when someone has offended or wronged them. While hurt feelings may tempt you to pay someone back for what she did, don't do it. Instead, as a follower of Jesus, forgive her and try to be kind to everyone.

Sarah was hurt and angry when her best friend invited another girl to spend the night, but didn't include Sarah. On Monday she heard the other girl talking about all the fun they'd had, going to a movie, ice-skating at the rink, and making fudge. Sarah fumed all week, although she pretended to her friend that she didn't mind. But Sarah wanted revenge. She intended to pay her friend back by doing the same thing to her, only Sarah would make sure she planned even MORE fun things to do.

Sarah had fallen into a tempting trap. Getting revenge led her into a worse kind of slavery than being stuck in her hurt feelings. She became bitter and sarcastic with her friend, trying to wound her as she'd been wounded. Sarah ended up killing the relationship.

God doesn't want that for you. When friends disappoint you, go first to God with your hurt feelings. Ask for his help to forgive your friend. Talk about it with a parent. Then go to your friend and talk about the situation. There may be reasons for her actions you know nothing about.

Retaliation is never a Christian choice. Christians are called to forgive. "Do not say, 'I'll pay you back for this wrong!' Wait for the LORD, and he will deliver you" (Proverbs 20:22 NIV).

Give up the idea of paying someone back. Let the Lord free you instead.

Did You Know ...

that you're supposed to do good to your enemies without expecting anything back? That's what God does, and it's what we're supposed to do, hard as it may be! Read Luke 6:35.

More To Explore: Leviticus 19:18 and Proverbs 25:21

Girl Talk:

Have you ever wanted revenge when someone hurt you? What did you do about it? Did it help or make the situation worse? Did you talk to God about it?

God Talk:

"Lord, getting revenge is so tempting. I know it's not right, and I need your help to let go and forgive. Please help me to follow your example. Thank you. Amen."

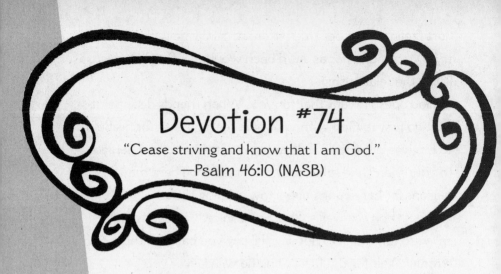

Devotion #74

"Cease striving and know that I am God."
—Psalm 46:10 (NASB)

Settle Down

When times are frightening and our world is falling apart, the Lord tells us to calm down. We are to stop spending so much energy on figuring out what to do. He says to be silent, to be still. Remember that he is almighty God, and he has everything under control.

Kaitlyn forgot to padlock her locker, and now her new running shoes are missing. Her mom saved for weeks to buy those shoes! She's been told a dozen times to lock up, but she was in a hurry this morning. Kaitlyn runs to the principal's office first, but they aren't in the Lost and Found. She checks all the hallways and restrooms, hoping they've been tossed somewhere. She throws everything out of her locker onto the floor, hoping they are buried under the clutter. She's near tears. Now what is she going to do?

When you're upset or angry or in pain, it takes faith to be quiet and concentrate instead on God's power to save you. Stretch your faith muscle, and think on the good things of God and how he's solved your problems in the past. "Meditate within your heart on your bed, and be still" (Psalm 4:4 NKJV).

Part of being still and knowing that he is God is trusting in a good outcome. If God is permitting problems or a crisis into our lives, he has a purpose. And if we trust him through it, he will make it all work out for our good. "We know that in all things God works for the good of those who love him, who have been called according to his purpose" (Romans 8:28 NIV).

The next time a problem hits you, *stop*. Don't wear yourself out running around. Get quiet instead. Let God speak to you and help you.

Did You Know ...

that several psalms talk about meditating on God's Word and all the things he's done? Think about how much God does every day, to remind yourself that he will take care of you too. Read Psalms 48:9; 77:12; and 119:48.

More To Explore: Psalm 100:3 and Job 37:14

Girl Talk:

When you're upset, how do you act? Do you panic and have outbursts, or do you talk with God? Don't waste energy on emotions that get you nowhere!

God Talk:

"Lord, I sometimes panic when things go wrong. I want to be calm. Please help me go to you first for help and patience. Thank you for your perfect example. Amen."

Devotion #75

"We know and rely on the love God has for us. God is love. Whoever lives in love lives in God, and God in him." —1 John 4:16 (NIV)

Living To Love

We know how much God loves us. We trust in that and lean on him. God is love! Believers live in God, and he lives in them. True followers have the habit of loving others. Kate tried to be loving, but it was so hard. She would promise herself not to snap at her brother, but she still did it. She made lists—like New Year's resolutions—of nice things she was going to do. More often than not, she didn't do them. She was trying to be loving in her own strength and finding it impossible.

Love is more than an emotion we feel toward another person or some kind act we do. To truly love is to have God work through our lives. If you're a believer, then God lives in you. And God *is* Love. So God is patient, God is kind, he does not brag, he endures things, he believes all things, he is full of hope, and God never fails. (See 1 Corinthians 13:4–8.) As we ask him to work in us and love others through us, we will begin to see the very same characteristics become true in our lives. God is Love, and that's why "Love never fails" (1 Corinthians 13:8 NKJV).

First John 3:16 (NLT) says, "We know what real love is because Christ gave up his life for us. And so we also ought to give up our lives for our Christian brothers and sisters." You may never have to physically die for anyone, but loving others will cause other things in you to die. You may have to die to selfishness, a short temper, or backbiting—any habit that prevents you from truly loving others.

God lives in you. Lean on that love, and spread it to others!

Did You Know ...

that we're called God's children because he loves us so much? Parents have so much love for their children, but God has so much *more* love even than our parents! Read 1 John 3:1 for assurance.

More To Explore: Psalm 36:7–9 and 1 John 3:24

Girl Talk:

How hard (or easy) is it for you to be loving? Do you have bad habits that need to die?

God Talk:

"Lord, I know that you are love. Help me to be more loving, just as you love me. Thank you for your perfect example. Amen."

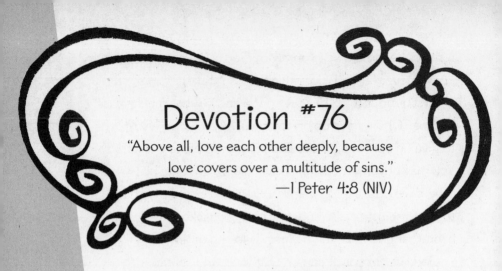

Devotion #76

"Above all, love each other deeply, because
love covers over a multitude of sins."
—I Peter 4:8 (NIV)

Love Is Patient, and Not Easily Angered

Love is shown in actions. Instead of picking at people's every fault, overlook them. (You like it when others overlook your minor failures.) No one is perfect, and love shows that by being patient with others' weaknesses.

Maria and Rebecca were good friends and partners in their science project. Rebecca got down to work immediately every time they met, but Maria had a tendency to chatter while she worked. Rebecca found it annoying because Maria made mistakes and wasted time that way. Rebecca mentioned it, and Maria tried to curb her talking. Sometimes she succeeded, but often she failed. Rebecca valued her friendship with Maria, so she chose not to nag her about it.

Rebecca is a good example of "covering over many sins." This verse is part of Peter's letter talking to Christians who are truly trying, day by day, to improve their relationships with God and people. Even when we try hard, we will have failures. So will others. "Covering over many sins or failures," means having a patient or tolerant attitude toward the mistakes of others. The aim of this verse is to avoid trivial picking at tiny faults or weaknesses in others.

However, this verse does NOT mean that you cover up serious sins or criminal acts, such as physical beatings and sexual abuse. Love expects responsible behavior from others. Covering up such acts allows the irresponsible person to continue his very wrong actions. Whether it is happening to you or to someone else, report it. Don't cover it up.

We all have minor faults and weaknesses we're trying to conquer. We appreciate it when others are kind to us and understand our failures. Give that same love and understanding to others.

Did You Know ...

that the famous "Love Chapter," 1 Corinthians 13, talks about the fact that love always protects? Love has many aspects to it. Read especially 1 Corinthians 13:4–7.

Girl Talk:

Think of the friend you spend the most time with. Is there a habit of hers that you don't mention because you love her? Do you have any habits that she lovingly doesn't mention?

More To Explore: Proverbs 10:12; 17:9

God Talk:

"Lord, I know I'm not perfect. Please help me to be loving in the way I deal with bad habits or something that bugs me. Help me to know whether to say anything or not. Thank you for being the perfect model of love! Amen."

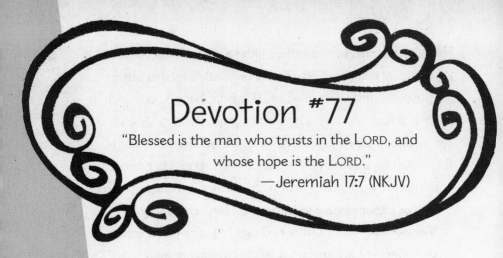

Devotion #77

"Blessed is the man who trusts in the LORD, and
whose hope is the LORD."
—Jeremiah 17:7 (NKJV)

Lean on The Lord

A girl who trusts in the Lord will be happy, bliss-
ful, and full of good fortune. Trusting the Lord
includes leaning on and relying on the Lord—not
people—for her supply of hope and self-confidence and
acceptance.

Trust can be hard. Do you have trouble trusting other
people? Have people mistreated you, or let you down, or broken their promises to you? Maybe they overlooked you when
you needed attention. How did that make you feel? Being mistreated and ignored can make us overly sensitive later in life. If
you feel destroyed emotionally when your friend doesn't
compliment you on your new dress, her opinion is too
important. If you're depressed for weeks when someone doesn't invite you to a party, your hope is in
the wrong place. You're using other people's
reactions to you to define who you are. If
you look to others to let you know if
you're "okay" or "acceptable," you will
constantly need to be working for their
love and approval.

If you have learned to trust in other people for your self-worth, it's time to shift that trust to God. If we trust in him, we won't be let down. Even the most loving parents or devoted friends will let us down sometimes. They're human, not perfect. But believers can trust God for their self-esteem. We can count on him to see us through any pain or difficulty we're in. No matter how much you love other people, keep your total trust in God alone. "The LORD God, my God, is with you. He will not fail you nor forsake you" (1 Chronicles 28:20 NASB).

Trust in the Lord. Put your hope in him. He will never, *ever* let you down.

Did You Know ...

that you are blessed if you take refuge in the Lord? See Psalm 146:5 for your assurance.

God Talk:

"Lord, I know I put too much importance on what others think of me. Help me to think only of what you think of me. I want to be more like you. Thank you. Amen."

More To Explore: Psalm 32:10

Girl Talk:

When you do something, do you think about what your friends will say? How often do you think about what God will say?

Devotion #78

"Now I am coming to You; I say these things while I am still in the world, so that My joy may be made full and complete and perfect in them [that they may experience My delight fulfilled in them, that My enjoyment may be perfected in their own souls, that they may have My gladness within them, filling their hearts]."
—John 17:13 (AMP)

I've Got The Joy, Joy, Joy ...

Jesus is talking here to his Father, God, about his disciples. (If you're a believer, that's you too!) Jesus said he taught his followers how to live so they could be happy. Jesus wants you to have "gladness" filling your heart and joy flooding your soul (which is your mind, your will, and your emotions).

Some days are easy to feel joy. Your homework gets an A. Your hair behaves. Your little brother is staying overnight with a friend. But what about the days you fall in the mud, you forget your homework, and you're grounded for hogging the phone? Can you have joy on those days? Believe it or not, yes, you can. Your joy comes from the Lord, not from your circumstances.

One reason Jesus wants you to be filled with joy is that he loves you. Another reason is that joy makes you strong! "Do not sorrow, for the joy of the LORD is your strength" (Nehemiah 8:10 NKJV). Satan delights in stealing your joy because it also steals your strength and makes you weak. When you're weak, it's easier for Satan to tempt you and discourage you. When you're weak, you probably won't be sharing the good news with others either.

Understand this: *it is God's will for you to enjoy life!* "This is the day the LORD has made; let us rejoice and be glad in it" (Psalm 118:24 NIV).

Did You Know ...

that even King David had to work on having joy at all times? In Psalm 42, he says that his soul is downcast, but he will still praise his Savior and Lord.

Girl Talk:

Who gets the credit when you have good days? Who do you usually blame for the bad days? How can you remember to have joy *every* day?

More To Explore: John 15:9–11 and Romans 14:16–18

God Talk:

"Lord, I want to be filled with joy. Please show me anything that Satan is using to steal my joy. I want to love my life on good days and bad. Thank you. Amen."

Devotion #79

"I have told you these things, so that in me you may have peace. In this world you will have trouble. But take heart! I have overcome the world."
—John 16:33 (NIV)

When Trouble Comes

Jesus overcame every trouble he encountered in his life on earth. He even overcame death! If you're a believer, Jesus lives in you, and you have this very same power. So you can be at peace, even though you will face trials and sorrows in this life. Cheer up and take courage!

Trouble comes in all shapes and sizes. You might have people problems: your best friend moved, or the bully in gym class stole your shoes. You might have money troubles sometimes: you can't afford to join your friends at the water park, or your family's been evicted from your apartment for not paying the rent. The size or the shape of your problem doesn't matter though. If Jesus lives in you, you can overcome it.

Sometimes people are told that if they just accept Jesus as their Savior, all their problems will be over. The Bible clearly teaches that is not so. Jesus told his disciples that they *would* have troubles, but not to be discouraged by them. They could lean on him and overcome them. God uses the trials and tests in our lives to teach us valuable things, like patience and endurance and the power of prayer. We wouldn't develop these necessary qualities if life were smooth all the time.

Jesus said, "Peace I leave with you; my peace I give you. I do not give to you as the world gives. Do not let your hearts be troubled and do not be afraid" (John 14:27 NIV). So be at peace. Have courage. Then overcome every trouble that comes your way.

More To Explore: Ephesians 2:13–14

Did You Know ...

that it was common in biblical times to end letters with messages of peace? Philippians 4:6–7 is still often used today, as a benediction at church services. See 2 Thessalonians 3:16 for another peaceful ending.

Girl Talk:

When you talk to God about your problems, do you ask them to be taken away? Or do you ask God to help you through them?

God Talk:

"Lord, it is tough to get through problems. Please give me patience and peace as I give my troubles to you. Thank you for always being with me. Amen."

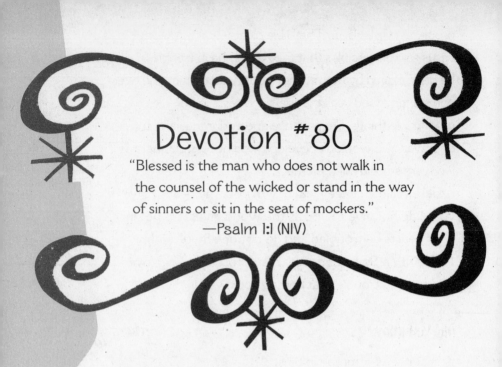

Devotion #80

"Blessed is the man who does not walk in the counsel of the wicked or stand in the way of sinners or sit in the seat of mockers."

—Psalm 1:1 (NIV)

Watch Where You Walk

You will have a happy life if you respect God's laws and obey them. But you must avoid arranging your life according to what mockers teach. They laugh at God's laws and defiantly reject his ways. Don't take advice from such people. Don't even hang around with those who make sinful behavior a way of life.

Some mockers are easy to spot, and therefore easy to avoid. They sneer when you mention church. They swear using God's name as a curse word. They do whatever they please as their way of life.

However, some who reject God's laws aren't so easy to identify.

Jill was bitter about her parents' divorce, and nothing her mom or dad could say made any difference. When she confided her hateful feelings to her best friend at church, her friend said, "What they did was terrible. Look how it's affected your life! You've had to move, your mom has no money, and you're gone all the time on visitations. If you forgive them, they'll think what they did is all right with you." Jill's friend meant well in her sympathy, but her advice classifies her as a "mocker." She is disrespecting much of God's Word that commands us to forgive (Matthew 6:14–15; 18:21–22; 2 Corinthians 2:7; and many more).

When situations come up, many voices will tell you what you should do. Listen to only the voice that tells you to obey God's written Word. When God's will becomes the most important thing to you—when you choose to follow God's Word and nothing else—mockers will soon no longer be walking with you.

Walk on the narrow path defined by God's Word, and watch how joyful your life becomes!

Did You Know ...

that you can't just know what the Bible says, you have to live it? Jesus says several times that you will be blessed if you do what the Word of God says. Read Luke 11:28 and John 13:15–17.

More To Explore: Proverbs 13:20

Girl Talk:

Who do you ask for advice? Are they Christians? Do they give the advice that God would give? Do you ask him directly for help?

God Talk:

"Lord, I get all kinds of advice about everything. Please help me to know whose advice to follow. Help me to come to you first, always. Thank you for always being there for me. Amen."

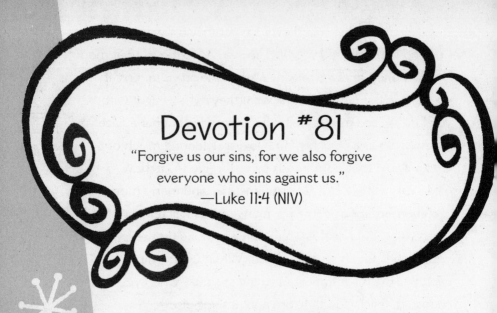

Devotion #81

*"Forgive us our sins, for we also forgive
everyone who sins against us."*
—Luke 11:4 (NIV)

The Freedom of Forgiveness

When we forgive, we give the other person freedom, just as God gives us freedom from the shame and
guilt of our own sins. When we forgive, we give up our
"right" to pay someone back for what they did to us.

Kyla endured physical beatings when her dad came home
drunk from the bar; they didn't stop until the school nurse
spotted the bruises and reported it. A neighbor boy was
molesting Britney after school until her mom caught him and
turned him over to the police. Should these girls forgive
their abusers? Believe it or not, yes.

However, we need to understand what forgiveness
is—and what it *isn't*. Forgiveness is NOT:

- Pretending that something bad didn't
  happen.
  - Pretending that what happened
    wasn't so bad after all.
  - A quickie shortcut to get rid of hurt
    feelings.

Forgiveness IS:

- Letting go of getting even.
- Putting the responsibility for what happened on the abuser's shoulders, where it belongs.
- Giving your hurt to God so he can begin the healing.

It may take a long time, and you may need help to do it, but (for your own sake) forgive the person who abused you. It does NOT make what they did to you okay. They will still have consequences for their behavior. If they broke the law, they may go to jail. If they damaged you, they may have to leave the home until they've had enough help to be safe again. Forgiving someone just means you have given up your right for revenge. You release your hurt and bitterness, and you let God (and maybe the courts) deal with that person.

Forgive—and set your*self* free.

Did You Know ...

that Joseph forgave his brothers and saved their lives, even though they had sold him into slavery years before? Read Genesis 45.

More To Explore: Ephesians 4:31–32

Girl Talk:

Have you ever had a bad experience that needs forgiveness? Do you wonder sometimes if it was really your fault? Have you asked God to heal you?

God Talk:

"Lord, you know I was deeply hurt by _____. Please help me to really forgive and let go of this hurt. I know it wasn't my fault. Please heal me, Lord. Thank you. Amen."

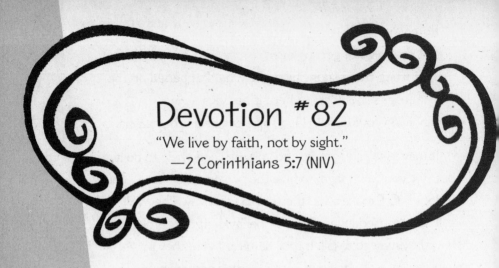

Devotion #82

"We live by faith, not by sight."
—2 Corinthians 5:7 (NIV)

Faith in His Word

We base our actions and our lives on what we believe, not what we can see with our eyes or experience with our senses. Instead of magnifying our circumstances, we should focus on the truth in God's Word. Do you feel frustrated with your math homework? No matter how hard you work, the answers are wrong. Do you decide you just can't do it? Or are you in a relationship with an angry person? Have you decided that you can't help it if all your conversations turn into fights? That may be how you *feel*, but it's not what God's Word says.

Your homework is so hard you can't do it? Truth: "I can do everything through him who gives me strength" (Philippians 4:13 NIV). God's Word says you can lean on his strength and power to get the job done.

Your conversations with that angry person have to end up in fights? Truth: "A gentle answer turns away wrath, but a harsh word stirs up anger" (Proverbs 15:1 NIV). God's Word says if you answer him with a gentle answer, it will turn aside his anger.

Are you going to believe what you see with your eyes and experience with your emotions? Or are you going to believe what God says in his Word? Remember, "God is not a man, that he should lie" (Numbers 23:19 KJV). His Word is the absolute truth.

Your problems may not disappear overnight. God may seem slow in coming to the rescue, but he uses the waiting time to stretch your faith and encourage you to be steady in prayer. "We fix our eyes not on what is seen, but on what is unseen. For what is seen is temporary, but what is unseen is eternal" (2 Corinthians 4:18 NIV).

Trust God, and live according to your belief in him.

Did You Know ...

1 Corinthians 13:12 says that right now, we "see in a mirror dimly," but in heaven, we will see face-to-face? Paul is telling us that we can't know everything yet—that's part of having faith. Later, in heaven, we will see the whole, clear picture.

Girl Talk:

How often do you let your feelings rule your actions? Do you ever convince yourself of something because that's what you really "feel"?

More To Explore: Hebrews 11:1 and Romans 8:24-25

God Talk:

"Lord, I let my feelings get the better of me sometimes. Please help me to go to you first. I want my actions to reflect you. Thank you. Amen."

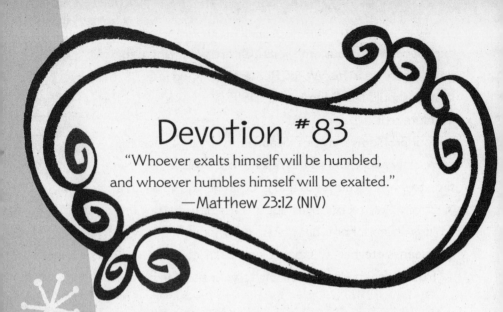

Devotion #83

"Whoever exalts himself will be humbled,
and whoever humbles himself will be exalted."
—Matthew 23:12 (NIV)

What Goes Up, Must Come Down

You have two choices. You can praise and promote
and honor yourself. If you do, your condition will be
brought back down by force or by discipline. On the other
hand, if you will humble and restrain yourself, God will lift
you up. He will honor you when the time is right.

Maddie bragged continually about her private voice lessons
and told everyone she'd get the lead in the school musical.
She was so sure she'd win the part that she bought special
costumes and memorized the heroine's lines. She said she
hoped Leah got a chorus part because Leah's voice
would make good background music for Maddie's
solo. When the cast list was posted, however,
Leah had the lead and Maddie was on the
scenery crew. Maddie's voice was excep-
tional, but her attitude of superiority
cost her the part she wanted.

Being puffed up with pride is a big deal
with God. Pride turned Lucifer, a beautiful

angel, into Satan, the devil. Being humble is being able to see yourself through God's eyes. Humility is not thinking you're a no-good worm. After all, we're made in God's very own image. But we are also to hold others up higher and not have an overly exalted opinion of ourselves. Pride and humility cannot live in the same heart. We can confess the pride and get rid of it. Or we can puff ourselves up with pride, and then endure the painful consequences when God corrects us. "Pride goes before destruction, and a haughty spirit before a fall" (Proverbs 16:18 NKJV).

Have healthy self-esteem, but remain humble. Wait for God to lift you to a place of importance when the time is right. He will!

Did You Know ...

that Jesus says we need to be like little children to enter the kingdom of heaven? He means that children are trusting and humble. Read Matthew 18:1–4.

More To Explore: James 4:6–7

Girl Talk:

How often do you talk about yourself to others? Do you brag about your talents? Or do you give God the credit?

God Talk:

"Lord, I know you have given me talents to use. Please help me to be humble and use my talents for your glory. Thank you for all that you see in me. Amen."

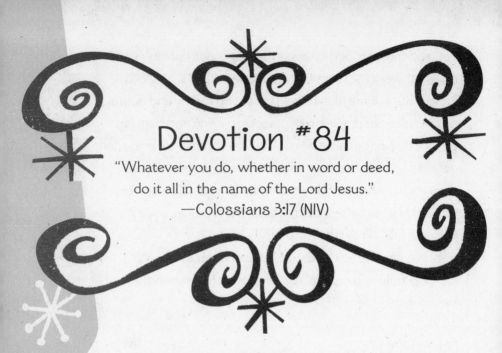

Devotion #84

"Whatever you do, whether in word or deed,
do it all in the name of the Lord Jesus."
—Colossians 3:17 (NIV)

For ALL The RighT Reasons

In the words you say or the things you do, remember
that you represent the Lord. Say and do things for the right
reasons, with godly motives.

Cara and Nicole were friends at church, and they decided to
babysit during the summer. Cara took care of two preschoolers
while their single mom worked. This mom couldn't pay as
much, but she let Cara take the children to summer Bible
school. Nicole babysat for another family. They had a pool,
money for ordering pizzas, and a big-screen TV. Nicole
thought she'd have more fun working for this family. Which girl do you suppose is babysitting in
the name of the Lord?

Why do you do the things you do?
Why do you say the things you say? Is it
because you want others to feel the love
of God flowing through you to them? Or,
if you look deeper, might you find another

reason? Maybe you say a kind word or do a favor for someone to gain their approval, or so they won't be mad at you. (Would Jesus do it for those reasons?) Maybe you do something, like babysit for your aunt, because you feel like you have no choice. These are not good motives. Remember, "whatever you do, do it heartily, as to the Lord and not to men" (Colossians 3:23 NKJV). Don't look to people for a reward for good deeds, but look to God to bless you.

Check your motives. Do the right things for the right reasons.

Did You Know ...

that Hezekiah prospered because he obeyed God's commands and worked "wholeheartedly"? Read 2 Chronicles 31:20–21.

Girl Talk:

Why do you do things? Do you figure out what you can get out of it before you agree? Do you ask God what you can do for him?

More To Explore: 1 Corinthians 10:31 and 1 John 3:18

God Talk:

"Lord, it's easy to do things for my benefit. Please help me to do tasks for your sake. I want to help others in order to lift you up, not me. Thank you for reminding me why I should do things. Amen."

Mini-Quiz:

1. **T / F** Obedience should come from the heart. (Colossians 3:22)

2. **T / F** The wrong motives get you what you ask for. (James 4:3)

3. **T / F** A man's motives seem innocent to him, but the Lord knows the truth. (Proverbs 16:2)

1. T   2. F   3. T

Devotion #85

"None of these things move me; nor do
I count my life dear to myself, so that
I may finish my race with joy."
—Acts 20:24 (NKJV)

Run With Joy

The apostle Paul had endured many hardships (beatings, shipwrecks, being in prison), yet he said those things didn't change his direction or purpose in life. He was even ready to die, if necessary. His only goal was to finish his race with joy. You may not face a shipwreck as you live your life, but you'll face other things. It could be the teacher who likes to embarrass you. Or maybe you're teased about being the tallest girl in your class. Maybe you have a parent who is never satisfied with anything you do, no matter how hard you try. These are hardships too.

How could Paul finish his race with joy, when it was filled with hardships? His secret is found in 2 Corinthians 12:10 (NIV): "That is why, for Christ's sake, I delight in weaknesses, in insults, in hardships, in persecutions, in difficulties. For when I am weak, then I am strong." How can that be possible? Because when Paul was weak, he leaned on God harder for help. He depended on God's strength to get the job done. And when you're filled with the strength of almighty God, that's strong!

So no matter what you're experiencing right now, you can do what Paul did. If you're filled with God's strength, you'll feel joy in your life and work, a joy that can't be explained. And when you've accomplished what you set out to do, you'll be able to say like Paul: "I have fought the good fight, I have finished the race, I have kept the faith" (2 Timothy 4:7 NKJV).

Complete your race with joy!

Did You Know ...

there are other verses that talk about our Christian faith as a race? Hebrews 12:1–2 talks about laying aside things that slow us down. First Corinthians 9:24–27 talks about running a race with purpose, not aimlessly.

More To Explore: 2 Corinthians 4:16–18; 7:4

Girl Talk:

How do you face hardships and problems? Do you grumble, or do you smile and praise God? It might be hard, but the prize at the end of this race is priceless!

God Talk:

"Lord, I know there will be times of trial in my life. Help me to stay joyful and remember that you're always with me. I want to depend only on you! Amen."

Devotion #86

"He who walks with wise men will be wise,
but the companion of fools will be destroyed."
—Proverbs 13:20 (NKJV)

The Right Friends Make ALL The Difference

If you make friends with those who exercise good judgment and common sense, you will learn to do the same. But if you choose fools for friends—those who lack good judgment—you will learn their ways instead. In the end, you will be defeated and ruined.

Before Amber moved, her closest friend, Carrie, lived next door. They studied together at night, and they quizzed each other before tests. They also ran a babysitting business and saved money to buy new bikes. At her new school, Amber's best friend was just as fun, but when they got together to study, Jasmine talked and flipped through fashion magazines or watched TV. Jasmine got a hefty weekly allowance, but it was always gone within a few days. Before long, Amber's grades slipped too. She cleaned out her savings account to buy clothes she didn't really want. Jasmine was a nice girl, but not a wise one. By being close friends with Jasmine, Amber had learned her undisciplined ways.

Some foolish friends are openly defiant as well. They cheat on schoolwork, they lie to their parents about where they're going, and they steal money from their dads' wallets. Avoid friends like this too! "Let no one deceive you with empty words, for because of such things God's wrath comes on those who are disobedient. Therefore do not be partners with them" (Ephesians 5:6–7 NIV).

Friends are one of God's greatest blessings in this life. They are meant to be enjoyed and treasured. However, you must choose your friends with care!

Did You Know ...

that King Rehoboam listened to his friends instead of the elders who helped his father, King Solomon? Read about the bad choice his friends led him to make in 1 Kings 12:1–14.

Girl Talk:

Think about your closest friends. Would God approve of how they live their lives? What do you do when you're with them? Sophie and the Corn Flakes make good choices when choosing friends. (Look for their lunch-table group in *Sophie's Secret*.)

More To Explore: 1 Corinthians 15:33–34

God Talk:

"Lord, having friends is important to me. Having friends who love you and act like it is even more important. Please help me to see their true colors. Thank you. Amen."

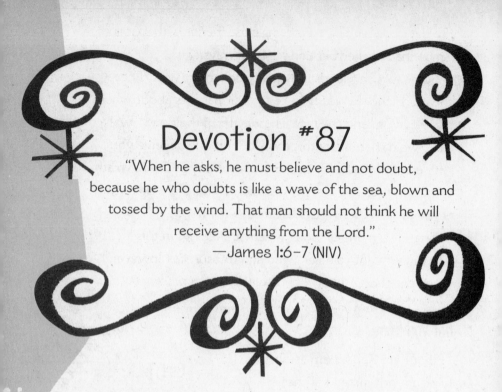

Devotion #87

"When he asks, he must believe and not doubt, because he who doubts is like a wave of the sea, blown and tossed by the wind. That man should not think he will receive anything from the Lord."
—James 1:6-7 (NIV)

Riding The Waves

In some hurtful or confusing situations, we don't know what to do. There isn't always a specific Bible verse that spells out our answer. However, we can always go to God for wisdom. You must believe in your heart that God hears you and will answer you. People who can't make up their minds—believing one minute, then doubting the next—are as unstable as the rolling waves of the sea. People like that should not expect to receive anything from the Lord.

Do you doubt God when a fearful thought crosses your mind? No. Satan tries to attack all believers with doubt. To know if you're really "double-minded," check what's coming out of your mouth. Do you sound like this? "I just know God heard my prayer. I'll be on the lookout for my answer . . . Boy, I don't know. It's taking a long time to get my prayer answered. I don't think God heard me or will help me." THAT'S doubt.

The one who gets her prayers answered, the Bible says, is the one who prays in faith. And after a time, when nothing seems to be happening, the words coming out of her mouth are still filled with faith: "I know God heard me. I know my answer is on its way. God's timing is perfect. He won't be late by a single hour." That's what faith is—believing even before circumstances match up. "Without faith it is impossible to please Him, for he who comes to God must believe that He is, and that He is a rewarder of those who diligently seek Him" (Hebrews 11:6 NKJV).

Believe God—and keep believing—when you pray. He'll never let you down.

Did You Know . . .

that Hebrews 10:23 says we must "hold unswervingly" to the hope we have? It means we must stay on course, no matter what. God will bring us through anything!

Girl Talk:

Do you ask God for help and leave your troubles in his hands? Or do you ask for help, but do your own thing anyway because you think it's better?

More To Explore: Ephesians 4:14–15 and Matthew 21:22

God Talk:

"Lord, I know I don't always wait for your answer. Please help me to have patience and to trust that you will come through for me. You always have; you always will! Thank you. Amen."

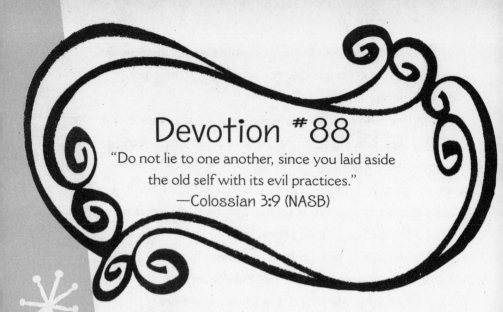

Devotion #88

"Do not lie to one another, since you laid aside
the old self with its evil practices."
—Colossian 3:9 (NASB)

Nothing But The Truth

Do not lie to one another. It doesn't fit who you are now. You've done away with your old self with its morally wrong practices.

Kylie paused the movie when the phone rang. "Hello?" She rolled her eyes when she heard it was Darla, the boring girl who lived two doors down. "Sorry, but I can't go to the pool," Kylie said. "I'm doing chores for my mom." She felt a twinge of guilt when she hung up, but lying seemed better than going to the pool with Darla or telling her she was boring.

Most of us think of ourselves as honest people, yet studies show that some of those who identify themselves as believers lie many times each day. Why do we do it, when we know that lying is wrong? Sometimes we don't want to be held responsible, so we hide behind made-up excuses. "I didn't have time to do it. I've been too busy!" (We don't add that we've been busy watching

TV and playing video games.) Or we lie to avoid discipline. "I didn't know it was due *today*." (Even though it's written in our planner.) Or we want to look good to someone else: "I like to wear the best. See my new TOMMY JEANS?" (We don't mention that we got them at Goodwill.)

Why is telling the truth so important in loving others? Because telling the truth builds trust, and lies destroy trust. Love and lies don't mix. If you love someone, you will tell them the truth. Telling the truth takes courage and confidence. It means taking a risk that someone will reject you for owning up to your failures or fears. Being completely honest isn't easy, but God's Word is clear: do not lie.

You're a new person now. Build trust with others by being truthful.

Did You Know ...

that the devil's native language is lying? John also calls him the father of lies. Read John 8:44.

God Talk:

"Lord, sometimes little lies seem to solve problems for me. Please help me to remember that the truth spoken in love is so much better than lies. I want to be a good model of you. Thank you. Amen."

More To Explore: Leviticus 19:11 and Zechariah 8:16

Girl Talk:

Think of the last time you told a little white lie. Do you think it solved the problem, or did it make the problem last longer? What could have been the benefit of telling the truth? What does God say to do?

Devotion #89

"We pursue the things which make for peace and
the building up of one another."
—Romans 14:19 (NASB)

Pursue Peace

We are to pursue the things that lead to peace and
building one another up. *Pursue* is a strong word, meaning
"to search, hunt for, or go after." Sometimes it takes hard
work to live in peace with people, but we are commanded to
make every effort to do so.

In Megan's history class, each student was to choose a person in history for an oral report presentation. Carrie discovered that Megan had chosen Betsy Ross, the same person
she was reporting on. She got upset and ran to the
teacher, demanding that Megan choose another
historical figure. Megan was then called to the
teacher's desk. She listened to Carrie's
complaint, but she'd already done a lot of
research for the report herself. Yet, she
knew she should make an effort to find
a peaceful solution. "We could choose
different parts of Betsy Ross's life to

report on," Megan suggested, "and then we could still use the same person." Carrie frowned and said, "Well, I get to report on how she made the first flag then." Megan nodded and said, "Okay. I have some books showing that flag, if you want them. I'll cover her childhood in my report."

"Behold, how good and how pleasant it is for brethren to dwell together in unity!" (Psalm 133:1 NKJV). Seeking peace and pursuing solutions that build up someone else will cost you something—usually having your own way. Choose your battles, the things you feel you must fight for. Few things are worth an all-out war.

Instead, "encourage each other and build each other up, just as you are already doing" (1 Thessalonians 5:11 NLT). God will reward you for it.

Did You Know ...

that Paul told the church in Philippi to "do nothing out of selfish ambition or vain conceit"? Paul also said to be humble and look to the interests of others. Read Philippians 2:1–4.

More To Explore: Psalm 34:14 and Romans 12:18

Girl Talk:

When you have a conflict with someone, how do you react? Do you need to win? Do you try to find a peaceful solution?

God Talk:

"Lord, it's hard to always keep the peace. I need your help to stay calm and find peaceful ways of doing things. Please help me stay humble. Thank you! Amen."

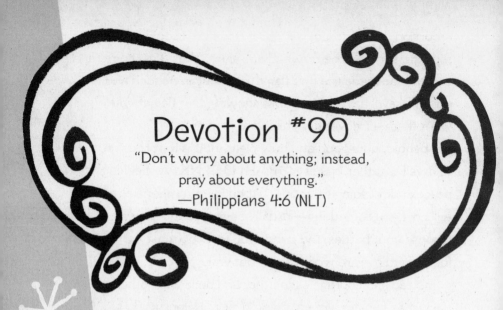

Devotion #90

"Don't worry about anything; instead,
pray about everything."
—Philippians 4:6 (NLT)

Don't Worry Away: Pray

As believers, we are not to be anxious or upset,
troubled or uneasy in our minds. How? Pray about
everything, and turn the situations over to God for help.
What do you catch yourself worrying about? Getting
lost when you start middle school? How your skin is breaking out? Taking swimming lessons when you're afraid of the
water? Wondering if your parents' frequent fighting is going
to end in divorce? Whatever your worries—no matter how
big—the answer is to pray instead of worry.

Easier said than done, right? Well, try these ways to
tame that worry habit:

- Separate "bad" worry from real concern.
  Decide if you can do anything about the
  situation. If so, write down a plan to
  handle it.
  - Don't worry alone. Talk to a friend,
    parent, teacher, youth leader, or
    counselor. You may receive helpful

advice. By talking it out, you may also discover solutions on your own that you couldn't see before.

- Take care of your body. We are more likely to worry when we're too tired, aren't eating healthy meals, and don't get enough exercise. Healthy bodies have minds that worry less.
- Look on the bright side. There is good in nearly every situation or person. Focus on that.
- Control your imagination. Don't get caught up in imagining all kinds of horrible "what-ifs." Our imaginations can take us from mild worry to a full-blown anxiety attack if we don't choose more realistic thoughts. Stick to what's happening right now—not what might happen in the future.
- Trust God. Whatever situation you're facing, invite God into the middle of it. You and God make an unbeatable team.

Worry is a bad habit, but trusting God can become a habit too. So tame that worry habit, and live a life filled with peace.

Did You Know ...

that Sophie worries a lot about her place in her family in *Sophie's Secret*? Read to find out how she handles worry.

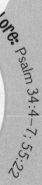

More To Explore: Psalm 34:4–7, 55:22

Girl Talk:

When you have a worry, what do you tend to do? Does worry take over your life, or do you give it to God and get on with living?

God Talk:

"Lord, there's always something I can worry about. Please help me to come to you first, giving you all my worries. Thank you for always taking care of me. Amen."

faiThGirLz!

Faithgirlz!™—Inner Beauty, Outward Faith

Sophie's World (Book 1)
Written by Nancy Rue
Softcover 0-310-70756-0

Sophie's Secret (Book 2)
Written by Nancy Rue
Softcover 0-310-70757-9

Sophie and the Scoundrels (Book 3)
Written by Nancy Rue
Softcover 0-310-70758-7

Sophie's Irish Showdown (Book 4)
Written by Nancy Rue
Softcover 0-310-70759-5

Sophie's First Dance? (Book 5)
Written by Nancy Rue
Softcover 0-310-70760-9

Sophie's Stormy Summer (Book 6)
Written by Nancy Rue
Softcover 0-310-70761-7

No Boys Allowed: Devotions for Girls
Written by Kristi Holl
Softcover 0-310-70718-8

Available now or coming soon to your local bookstore!

Zonderkidz.

faiThGirLz!

Faithgirlz!™–Inner Beauty, Outward Faith

COMING SOON

Sophie Breaks the Code (Book 7)
Written by Nancy Rue
Softcover 0-310-71022-7

Sophie Tracks a Thief (Book 8)
Written by Nancy Rue
Softcover 0-310-71023-5

Available now or coming soon to your local bookstore!

We want to hear from you. Please send your comments about this book to us in care of zreview@zondervan.com. Thank you.

Zonder**kidz**®

Grand Rapids, MI 49530
www.zonderkidz.com